Praise for *You Must Become A Tr*

"I started to read the book 'You Must Become a Trainer' as my personal development exercise for the week and it has become one of the best decisions I have made in the past few weeks. This book is a page-turner that is very instructive, timely and an answer to my prayers in the past few months. As a younger "sister", I have watched BJ practice each of the principles he shared in this book and equally shared in the proceeds of his success over the years. I highly recommend this book to every expert who needs to take their game to the next level, and like he said in the book "Do not sit on your gold mine of expertise, hoping the future will take care of itself. Start long before you need to start!"

Olusola F. Sotunde RD (NGA) M.Sc PhD, CEO/ Senior Technical Advisor Nutrition & Health, Beth Davids International, Ottawa, Canada

"Congratulations. I just read the first chapter and it is mind-blowing as usual. Wow! Thank you for sharing!"

Lara David Odufuwa, Human Resources Advisor, Canadian Mental Health Association

"The book is a comprehensive summary of steps in growing anyone desiring to step up his/her game as a highly focused and value-adding trainer. It is teaching me how to be more focused to overcome the obstacles that have been hindering my growth as a trainer."

Steve Oboh, CEO & Principal Trainer, Stevebeck Limited

"Bolaji's book, 'You Must Become a Trainer' is indeed an absolute gem.

Very few people have had the ability to influence my thinking but the persuasive and easy to read style, laced with hard-earned insights makes it a convincing guide for leveraging my expertise for commercial benefit. From understanding why expertise is so vital and how one can profit from it to why it's important for one to niche and become an expert at what you do to earn respect and profit from your craft, the time invested to read this book, is well worth it. The most insightful take away is how he manages to crystallize the contrast between being in employment and still managing to establish channels for earning passive income by leveraging your expertise. His deep understanding of the subject and practical experience in this field makes this book a definite game-changer for all professionals."

Olasunkanmi Adenuga, Director of Learning, Digital Learning Africa

"We all have intense levels of potential in our minds screaming for exposure, but we barely harness them into being our competitive advantage. I, for instance, always end up embracing degrading elements such as postponing or thinking that am not equal to the task. 'You Must Become a Trainer' was suggested to me by a friend who had gained so much from the author and I decided to give it a try and see how it would impact my leadership role in a new startup I was heading.

The book was inherently informative and the author provides a foolproof recipe on how to leverage our skills and knowledge to make our lives better and gain a competitive advantage. What I loved most is how the ideas discussed are based on practical techniques and written in a flow that is easy to comprehend. The book has taught me so much as a leader and entrepreneur, and I am certainly going to get a few copies and distribute them to my fellow leaders in the startup. I believe that those seeking enlightenment on how to harness their abilities and successfully embrace entrepreneurship will find a gem out of this book.

Yes, the book is worth every penny and it was such a valued read. It is an amazing job you did there, Bolaji!"

Mary Heist, Director of Business Administration, Wellington at Hershey's Mill, USA

"Definitely 5 stars! I wish Bolaji had written this book 25 years earlier so I could have avoided some of the mistakes I've made...

With the rapidly changing business terrain, the traditional ideology for success that is built around preparing yourselves to be 'employable for life' is clearly under threat. The counter argument encourages us to 'gear up' to be masters of our own destinies, rather than viewing our income as someone else's responsibility.

'You Must Become a Trainer' makes a compelling argument for millions of subject matter experts either longing to leave the 9-5 grind or create supplementary income to explore the immense benefits of transitioning into professional training. The book asks thought provoking questions designed to transform the readers mindset while also providing practical insights and easy to apply tools with each chapter.

The best part of this book is that it uses real life examples from Bolaji's actual experience to provide an easy to understand, pragmatic and believable framework for experts from any profession to leverage what they already have (their education, expertise and experience) to get what they want.

If you are one of the millions of experts who have worked hard to attain mastery in their profession, but struggling to translate their expertise into notable income, impact and recognition, then 'You Must Become a Trainer' is a must read for you.

Foluso Aribisala, CEO, Workforce Group

"'You Must Become A Trainer: How to leverage your expertise, experience and education in any field to do what you love, impact lives, create wealth and own your future' encourages professionals to carve out a niche for themselves and improve their income-generating capabilities within this "new normal" paradigm.

This edu-inspirational book has three parts, and eleven chapters which all come together as a personal growth strategy playbook for trainers.

It is also a very timely book, as the world grapples with a recession caused by the global pandemic. The author opines that there are opportunities within the present daunting world and encourages these with quotes from great leaders such as Peter Drucker: "Today, knowledge has power. It controls access to opportunities and advancement."

If I have to find an error with the book, it's the title. Let's say it again. 'You Must Become A Trainer: How to leverage your expertise, experience and education in any field to do what you love, impact lives, create wealth and own your future' . No Bolaji, this could've been condensed. Your saving grace is that the narrative lived up to the title as it is indeed chock full of tips, advice, and informative material.

I would recommend this book to all professionals. It doesn't matter your career of choice, as the book centers on how to become a trainer using the knowledge you gained over the years. Have a read even if you are employed as multiple streams of income is the current necessity for survival."

Nzuri Shelley, Principal Creative Director, Golden designs, Jamaica

"An Excellent Guide

In 'You Must Become a Trainer', Bolaji Olagunju teaches the reader how to remain confident and find success, especially during these current hard times. Jobs are no longer secure, so one MUST find alternative sources of income.

Written from a very practical perspective, the author shared his personal stories which always ended with a valuable lesson. If you have a great knowledge base that you wish to share with others, then read this inspiring and well-written book. You can expect thorough explanations on how to create a new training business career and even though it might seem difficult at first e.g. for those that hate public speaking, the book contains tips to overcome all the hurdles that might hinder success.

Must read if you are really serious about becoming a successful trainer."

Beatriz Souza, Social Security Advocate, Portugal

"Once again, I am blown away by the author's ability to break down the most complex concepts into relatable and practical chunks of information.

From chapter 1, where he narrates his tale of stumbling into the training profession 'accidentally' to the very end where he proffers key success drivers for would-be trainers, this educational book is full of pragmatic advice delivered clearly, concisely and with a dash of his renowned wit and humor."

Apinke Ayodeji, Senior Marketing Manager, Golden Phoenix Publishing

"This book totally captured my attention. The writing style is clear, simple and point blank. It provides practical steps for building a solid training service company. Once in a while, a book is released to disrupt and re-direct the way we way we think, yearn, learn and earn. This is that book that shows the way to prosperity through training. Kudos!"

Chizor Wisdom Dike, President, Sustainable Development Academy

"'You Must Become a Trainer' is a must read for everyone. It came at the right moment when I am trying to find my purpose and see what problems I could solve that will empower me financially. Even in my busy schedule as a PhD student and Mum of 3 with no Nanny, I still read the first 100 pages within 3 days. God bless you for the insight I got."

Anyichie - Odis Adaora Isabella, Public Health Specialist

"This book has opened my eyes and has shown me that I have been doing most of the things in the wrong way. I always thought of trainers having to be teachers in the school or professors, but this book has completely changed my thinking.

Especially, I liked when the author shared the exercise for finding one's niche. Before now I used to struggle to focus on one particular skill area but now I know how best to approach and do things differently not just for my professional career but also in finding other side hustles. Highly recommended!"

Prateek Singh, Product Manager, Neshes Technology, UK

"I thought Bolaji's first book 'Hiring Right' was practical enough until I came across his second, 'You Must Become a Trainer'.

Without having finished reading, I already have ideas to implement.

Anyone that reads this and acts on the instruction will definitely make a significant impact in his/her chosen area of expertise."

Akindele Afolabi, Director, Workforce Assessment and Recruitment

"Any material from you sir is a must read for anyone interested in personal growth and enterprise development from a standpoint of relevant expertise. Thank you for sharing Bolaji Olagunju."

Gbenga Totoyi, Director, Membership and Market Development, CIPM Nigeria

"How many of us are trapped in unfulfilling jobs which sap our creativity, or find ourselves aiming for greatness only to get postponed or side tracked along the way? Often, we have all the tools we need to be successful but don't know how to use them effectively to give ourselves that competitive edge. You Must Become A Trainer is just the inspiration and guidance needed to understand how to utilise your skills and experience to take control of your future.

Throughout the book, the author illustrates his meaning through outlining his own experiences. Providing a practical, 'real world' application to what is being explained and making it easily understandable. I could relate to a lot of the issues and blocks discussed, personally I've always been a procrastinator and this has been holding my back for years. What really stood out for me is how these issues are addressed in an understanding but firm tone, making the reader feel inspired to take action and improve themselves.

This is a must-read if you are serious about making some big changes quickly, it doesn't pull any punches when it comes to getting you to take action and grow into the leader you always had the potential to be. If you want some insight and clarity into the path to successful entrepreneurship, this is the book to buy in 2020!"

Chelsea Barnes, Programmes Manager

"This book will absolutely blow your mind! Value adding from page 1! With many practical steps you can apply to your business / career. Too many lessons learnt... #YMBAT - "Start long before you need to start. Start when the stakes are not so high...this will give you a huge advantage and opportunity to build up necessary momentum...

Straight to the point and easy to understand. I was spellbound and couldn't drop the book once I started! I love Chapter 10: You must become a marketer! Yes! The book isn't just about training... You need to read this book! ...

Thank you Bolaji Olagunju #YMBAT – "There is no greater way to multiply your wealth than by increasing the number of people you impact through teaching them what you know."

Bose Oladehin, Lead Consultant, POD HR & Strategy

you **must**
become a
trainer

Also by Bolaji Olagunju

Hiring Right: A Matter of Life and Death for Businesses, Business Owners and Executives

https://hiringrightbook.com

you **must** become a trainer

How to leverage your expertise, experience and education in any field to do what you love, impact lives, create wealth and own your future

BOLAJI OLAGUNJU

Founder, Workforce Group and OwnersInstitute.com

Published by Lift Publishing

Copyright 2020 © Lift Publishing

Cover and interior design: Andy Meaden / meadencreative.com

Editor: Olawunmi Brigue

Hardcover ISBN: 978-1-7339779-6-8

Paperback ISBN: 978-1-7339779-5-1

Digital ISBN: 978-1-7339779-4-4

First edition, August 2020

DEDICATION

This book is dedicated to all our clients over the last sixteen years. Without you, we would not be where we are today as a business. Special thanks to these amazing individuals who took a chance on us and gave us the opportunity and platform to practise our craft and to learn, improve, add value and capture value in return; Mrs Ayo Jaiyesimi, Mr. Seyi Onajide, Mrs Morayo Oyeleke, Mr. Gbemiga Owolabi, Mrs Esther Akinnukawe, Mrs Ima Ofulue, Ms Irunna Ejibe, Mr Miyen Swomen, Mrs Chidinma Lawanson, Ms Lande Atere, Mr Obinnia Abajue, Mrs Amina Oyagbola, Mr. Dotun Adako, Mrs Temi Dalley, Mrs Ejemen Okojie, Mrs Funke Amobi, Mrs Kafilat Araoye, Ms Isioma Ogodazi, Mr Aruosa Osemwegie, Mr Funwa Akinmade, Mrs Patricia Aderibigbe, Mrs Tomilayo Esan, Mr Funso Tooki, Alhaji Ibrahim Jioril, Ms Kemi Onabanjo, Mr. Babatunde Jinadu, Mrs Banke Osunsanya, Ms Bolaji Agbede, Mrs Olanike Martins, Mrs Ifunanya Ekwueme, Mr. Eze Oseji, Mr. Femi Onanuga, , Mr. Gabriel Nwokeafor, Mrs Funmi Adegoke, H.E Mr Babajide Sanwo-Olu, Mr. Kunle Onabote, Mr. Lovell Omoanreghan, Mr Michael Owolabi, Mr. Morakinyo Oloyede, Mr. Ademola Aladekomo, Ms. Timipri Odu, Mrs Anu Ajayi, Mr. Muyiwa Olulaja, Mrs Nneka Okoro, Mr Jubril Aifolawe, Mrs Ivie Imasoge, Mr Nuru Adam, Dr Yomi Makanjuola, Mrs Ayo Ogunsanya, Mrs Ngozika Achebe, Mrs Roli Egbe, Mr Olakunle Olashore, Mr. Toye Thomas, Mrs Omayuli Wale-Ajayi, Mrs Osa Osowa, Mrs Abike Wesey Mr Oshoke Imoagene, Mrs Owen Omogiafo, Mrs Oyinyechukwu Kade, Mrs Oyiza Salu, Mrs Bukola Thomas, Mrs Tolulope Agiri, Nayo Ugoh, Mr Patrick Mbagwu, Mr Usen Udoh, Mrs Winifred Mena-Ajakpovi, Mr Oludare Sholajo, Mrs Stephanie Omobuwajo, Mr Bisi Ogunwoye, Mr Morakinyo Fadipe, Mr Kelechi Anukam, Mr Charles Nwachukwu, Ms Phil Oyawoye, Mr Ayoade Fadipe, Mrs Alaba

Femi-Johnson, Mrs Tosin Oyebola, Mr. Femi Enigbokan, Mr Azeez Omosun, Mrs. Adetokunbo Agbede Ayo-Ogunsanya, Mr. Seyi Oyesainu, Ms. Ayotunde Opeoluwa, Dr. Bashir Jamoh, Mr Jubril Saba, Mrs Adewunmi Oluremi, Mr Justus Aina, Mrs Tolulope Dayo-Peters, Mr. Kolawole Amusa, Mr. Seyi Oyesainu, Mrs Feyi Aina, Mrs. Bukola Kogbe, Mrs Grace Omo-Lamai, Mr Ephraim Osunde, Mrs Dorothy Tunde-Ajala, Mrs. Funlola Akintonde, Mr. Yomi Igbin and Mr Charles Udeozor.

This book is also dedicated to all lifelong learners everywhere in the world. You are the difference that makes all the difference. Your commitment to never-ending learning and improvement makes the world go round.

CONTENTS

FOREWORD xvii

PART 1   You Are Sitting on a Gold Mine 1

1 Ycu Must Make the Most of Your Expertise 3

2 You Must Secure and Own Your Future 11

3 You Too Can and Must Become a Trainer 25

4 12 Compelling Reasons Why You Must Become a Trainer ... 43

PART 2   Building Your Training Capabilities 65

5 You Must First Become a Student 67

6 You Must Select the Right Niche 79

7 You Must Design Your Training Program for Success ... 95

8 You Must Master the Art of Training Delivery 109

PART 3   Start Making Money as a Trainer 131

9 You Must Create a Sustainable Business Model 133

10 You Must Become a Marketer 145

11 You Must Create Your Online Course Empire 169

CONCLUSION   You Must Be the Best and Succeed 179

APPENDIX 1 – 101 Highly Interesting and Successful
Examples of Training Niches 187

APPENDIX 2 – Elizabeth's Lead Generating PDF:
The Key to Winning More Business (And Keeping It) 193

ABOUT THE AUTHOR 199

YOU **MUST** BECOME A **TRAINER**

FOREWORD

If you are looking to transition from a subject matter expert to a professional Trainer, this is the book for you. With an easy to apply framework and proven practical insights, this book will give you the tools needed for a seamless and successful transition.

My first set of role models were my schoolteachers, even though at the time, I would not have referred to them as such. I did not fully recognise until later in life, their passion, commitment and sacrifice in shaping me into who I am today, and who I am becoming. Through their teaching, they opened my eyes to a world of possibilities that transcended the classroom, and I believe this is one of the reasons I am so passionate about learning and teaching today. For this, I will always be grateful to them.

Bolaji has an uncanny ability to spot and spontaneously create teachable moments. Over the last decade, he has played the role of teacher and mentor to me and in my opinion, his never-ending compulsion to develop and empower others to fulfil their potential stands out amongst his many great attributes. This is arguably his biggest calling and will be one of his greatest legacies.

His new book, "You Must Become A Trainer" sits at the heart of his personal conviction that everyone has a God given responsibility to positively impact the lives of others by guiding, inspiring and empowering them to expand their dreams and fulfil their full potential.

The book particularly provides a compelling argument for subject matter experts in any field to leverage their expertise, experience, exposure, and education to explore the life changing opportunity that teaching provides. Bolaji provides practical, proven and easy to follow steps from over 20 years of hands on experience in designing and delivering high impact learning initiatives.

With the recent COVID-19 global pandemic and its adverse impact on livelihoods through a massive loss of jobs, there is no better time for subject matter experts to embark on this transition to become professional Trainers.

If you are one of the millions of experts who have worked hard to attain mastery in their profession, but are struggling to translate their expertise into notable income, impact and recognition, then "You Must Become A Trainer" is a must read for you.

Foluso Aribisala

CEO, Workforce Group

PART 1

YOU ARE SITTING ON A GOLD MINE

If you are a Subject Matter Expert but not a trainer, you might be missing the biggest opportunity of your life!

1

YOU MUST MAKE THE MOST OF YOUR EXPERTISE

"Never let a good crisis go to waste."
Winston Churchill

Things were looking up. The global economy had enjoyed a mini boom starting from the close of 2016 and leading into 2019. In the U.K., for example, consumer spending was performing better than expected and the jobs market was relatively stable, with employment rate near record levels and unemployment down to its lowest rate since the mid-1970s. [1]

And then, 2020 happened! We were barely two months into the year when COVID-19, an infectious disease caused by a newly discovered coronavirus, made its grand entrance. It spread like wildfire across global borders and brought the world to a complete standstill.

The last five months (March to July 2020) have been truly scary. We saw the pandemic hit on a global scale and almost overnight, the

---

[1] PWC's UK Economic Outlook. November 2019

world changed dramatically. As at the time of writing, there have been 19.5 million confirmed cases of COVID-19 with over three quarters of a million deaths. [2]

The economic impact has also been catastrophic. The stock market crashed. Businesses that had resiliently survived two world wars fell at the hurdle of the pandemic. The economic future of families all over the world was suddenly thrown into disarray as millions of people unexpectedly lost their jobs or lost their incomes for extended periods through being furloughed.

The unprecedented change the world has seen in such a short space of time is undoubtedly cause for serious concern. But it is also a source of anticipation and hope for people who know how to take full advantage of situations like this. Like the saying goes, "Never let a crisis go to waste." As this crisis ravaged the world, I kept asking myself, "What can I learn from this situation? What critical lessons does this crisis hold, and how should I respond? What are the implications for me, for my business, for the business community, for the clients I serve? How will this impact the future? How will this impact my ecosystem?"

During this crisis, my desperation to learn went into overdrive because I wanted to make sure that I did not let it go to waste.

"A pessimist sees the difficulty in every opportunity; an optimist sees the opportunity in every difficulty."
Winston S. Churchill

I have always prided myself on my love for learning. My commitment to continuous, never-ending learning and growth is unquestionable. During this crisis, my desperation to learn went into overdrive because I wanted to make sure that I did not let it go to waste. Consequently, I have learnt three extremely valuable lessons

---

[2] World Health Organisation

during this crisis. One, nobody knows anything for certain. Nobody. No one. Not the experts, not the scientists, not the business leaders, and most certainly not the politicians. I watched in sheer amazement as politicians came unhinged. World powers came unglued, and some of the most celebrated leaders went into panic mode, expressing the same kind of fears that I thought only small and medium sized business owners like me were dealing with. I watched an interview of a top CEO on CNN, and I was perplexed. The guy was fidgeting badly, and he downright looked scared. You could see the sheer panic written all over his face. He had no real answers for the questions presented to him. And he is not alone. We are all just making stuff up as we go. Everybody is just playing along with the system. So, I concluded that rather than be a victim of other people's gambling, I would instead take charge of my own future.

Two, it is now undoubtedly clear that relying on a job, an establishment, or on a single stream of income for financial security is extremely risky. COVID-19 has taught the world that diversification of income streams is the game-changing key to securing one's financial future. The way people panicked when they saw their job – their only source of income – vanish into thin air overnight, the fear I saw in people's eyes when they questioned what the future held for them, is an indication that it is time to take your future in your own hands. Now more than ever, people must come to terms with the fact that their best bet is to do everything within their power to own their future. Let me repeat that. You must accept the fact that you can no longer rely solely on establishments or on a job to secure your future. You must do everything within your power to create and own your own future. You owe it to yourself, your family, your community, and everybody around you.

> *You must do everything within your power to create and own your own future.*

And three, following the impact of COVID-19, any business – or individual – who does not own a stake in the online digital industry and does not claim their share of the stupendous amount of wealth being generated daily is doing themselves a great disservice. Having an online platform is no longer a nice to have. It is a must!

The question now is, how do you own your future? What steps can you take to increase your chances of long-term financial success? How do you beat the odds stacked up against you? Based on my personal experience and the experiences of thousands of people that I have interacted with over the years, I believe there is one unique and proven way to significantly increase your probability of building lasting wealth. And that is what this book is all about.

> *"The meaning of life is to find your gift. The purpose of life is to give it away."*
> Pablo Picasso

In our society today, there are millions of people who are sitting on gold mines. These people are knowledgeable experts who have worked very hard to attain mastery in their profession, but who are either struggling to realise their full potential or have found themselves boxed in by a ceiling that they cannot seem to break out of. A ceiling that has capped their influence and earning power at the same unsatisfactory level for a long time.

These experts are yearning for more. They know deep inside them that there is more. So, they are searching for the right opportunities to leverage the knowledge and experience they have amassed over the years to benefit themselves and others.

The desire to become more, to really do something of sizeable impact and perhaps, to leave a legacy, keeps them awake at night. Having built up so much intellectual property, they feel deeply frustrated that they could end up leaving the face of the earth without genuinely sharing their story, their experiences, and their expertise with the world in a way that would significantly improve people's lives and even impact nations. And to be able to achieve all these whilst doing very well for themselves financially.

On the other end, there are millions of people out there who desire growth and are reaching for the stars in their personal & professional lives. They are actively seeking the right knowledge, skills and expertise that would empower them to seize the opportunities in their paths. They observe established experts in their fields and wish they could emulate and follow their footstep. These people are thirsty not just for the knowledge the experts possess in abundance, but also for the training that only someone who has walked their path can provide.

However, there is a huge disconnect between the experts and the protégés. There is no clearly defined pathway for the two parties to connect. So, on one hand, you have experts who have all it takes – education, experience, exposure, expertise (what I call the 4Es) – to help protégés achieve their goals and desires, whilst making a living doing so (doing good whilst doing well).

On the other hand, there are individuals who are desperately in need of what the experts have to offer in order to realise their potential and fulfil their dreams, but they do not know how to access it. Their circle does not extend into the circle of influence they are aiming for and attempts to gain even a fleeting access to these experts have proved unsuccessful over and over again. The people they need to connect with in order to succeed in life, those who have established themselves as experts in their field, are way out of their reach. So, they resort to luck and uninformed hustle in trying to make their way to the top.

To give back is to pay forward. As an expert, you can do very well for yourself financially while spreading good to others by offering your expertise to the thousands of people that need it. It is not only the moral thing to do, but it can also be extremely rewarding financially and psychologically. This is what I hope this book will inspire you, the expert, to seek to achieve.

> *As an expert, you can do very well for yourself financially while spreading good to others by offering your expertise to the thousands of people that need it.*

I hope it will inspire everyone who has mastered any skill or competency to multiply their success by training others to do the same. I hope it will act as a bridge that will enable you, the expert, to build a platform that connects your expertise to those that need it and in doing so achieve your own dreams whatever they are – be it financial freedom, impact, influence or fulfilment.

The art of giving is supported by a universal law that says, the more you give, the more you get. The more people you influence, inspire and impact through creating training programs and online courses, the greater your financial rewards and the more secure your future will be. There is no greater way to multiply your wealth than by increasing the number of people you impact through teaching them what you know. It is better to teach someone to fish than to keep giving them fish. This is the law of stratospheric success.

I invite you to read this book if you desire to give back, for in giving back, you get more. Read this book and apply its principles if you wish to make an impact and leave a financial legacy for generations coming behind you. Read this book if you want to turn your expertise into your competitive advantage as you navigate an increasingly turbulent economic market. Read this book because you know you are simply too loaded to keep your expertise to yourself.

Do not allow fear or perfectionism hold you captive and prevent you from using your mind to create wealth. You must boldly step out and share your expertise with the world. You must diversify your income, impact a global community and own your future. You must become a trainer and online course creator.

KEY TAKEAWAYS

- The global COVID-19 pandemic took the world by storm and left colossal losses in its wake, including an economic crisis. But as Winston Churchill advised, "Never let a good crisis go to waste," you cannot sit idly and hope for the best (only to end up worse off). You must take decisive steps now to create an enviable future.

- The COVID-19 crisis has taught the world three lessons. One, nobody knows anything for certain, therefore you cannot entrust your future to a human being or an establishment, and you must take charge of it yourself. Two, relying on only one stream of income such as a salary is extremely risky. And three, digital technology has become the new way of life and anyone serious about financial wealth must claim a share of the ever-expanding trillion-dollar digital industry.

- The most fulfilling and profitable way to secure your financial future, impact lives and build a legacy is to leverage the education, experience, exposure, and expertise you have painstakingly accumulated over the years by becoming a Trainer. Through face-to-face trainings or online courses, you can become an instrument in other people's successes by teaching them what you know.

2

YOU MUST SECURE AND OWN YOUR FUTURE

"To stay ahead, you must have your next idea waiting in the wings."
Rosabeth Moss Kanter

"Bolaji, where are you? I have been trying to reach you all morning! Please call me!!!" That was one of several frantic voice messages a friend left for me one morning, a couple of years ago. I had been in an all-day strategy meeting with a client and had only just popped out for a few minutes to check my messages when I saw a barrage of missed calls and messages from him. And it was not even eleven o'clock in the morning yet. Had something terrible happened? I wondered.

I called him back straightaway and when he answered, the heightened urgency in his voice did nothing to allay my fears. He sounded confused, even desperate. This man, whom I had always known to be calm and composed in the way he approached everything was essentially reduced to a bag of nerves. Clearly, something was terribly wrong.

"Bolaji, I must see you." He insisted. "Can I come over and see you right away?" I looked at my watch. As much as I wanted to help, my meeting would go on for another four to five hours at least and unfortunately because I was leading the session, I could not just abandon it. I asked if we could talk over the phone, but he insisted that it had to be face-to-face. So, I gave him my earliest possible appointment and went back into the meeting room wondering what on earth could have gotten him so shaken up.

Barely an hour later, I received another phone call. This time it was from a lady I had mentored a few months prior to that. She too sounded worried and stressed, and she would not tell me over the phone why she needed to see me. What was immediately puzzling was that she worked for the same organisation as my friend who called me earlier that morning. I knew something was seriously wrong, but I did not know what it was. They both wanted to see me and would not tell me why. It was all very strange indeed!

By the end of that day, I had been contacted separately by three different people from that organisation. Three agitated phone calls. Same organisation.

It was not until later that afternoon when I discovered from another source what had happened. There had been a massive wave of layoffs at that organisation and two of the three people who reached out to me had lost their jobs. The third person had momentarily escaped but was deathly afraid that her name would appear on the next list.

Now that I knew what had happened, it was easy to see why they were all so disturbed. I wished it was a problem I could have dismissed with a casual wave of my hand and assured them that everything would be fine. But even I knew how serious the situation was. Even though it was pre-COVID, when the economy was certainly doing better than it is now, the jobs market simply did not elicit the kind of confidence that would make anyone think they could easily snap up a new job after being let go.

And to make matters worse, none of them had a backup plan or an alternative way to generate income. The layoff had suddenly put the two that were directly affected in an extremely vulnerable situation financially.

My first caller, in particular, was hit the hardest. Before that morning, he had been a highly paid manager in the bank, with a befitting lifestyle to go with it. He was married with four children and probably more worryingly, he was the sole earner in the family. His wife occasionally dabbled in business and brought in a bit of side income, but it was a mere drop in the bucket compared to their outgoings.

His children were in expensive private schools. He had a mortgage, car loans, and personal loans. And of course, he knew that it would not be long before missed bank payments unleashed a flurry of creditors threatening to take his home, his cars and whatever else had been mortgaged. He also had a host of extended family – parents, siblings, almost an entire village – who depended on him for financial sustenance.

So much was dependent on that job and having now lost it, the fear of losing all that was attached to it had become a real possibility. The world he once knew had crashed around him and the future looked bleak.

I wish I could say that his was an isolated case. But sadly, it is not. And, the sudden outbreak of COVID-19 has significantly compounded this problem. Millions of working professionals all over the world are dealing with unexpected job and income loss. Some will bounce back. But unfortunately, many will never regain the level of professional or financial success they enjoyed prior to the crisis. Unless, of course, they read this book and follow the advice I give in it.

Over the years, I have encountered many, many people who were hit hard by a sudden loss of income and never fully recovered. One person lost his high-profile managerial job and resorted to driving a taxi just to make ends meet. His children were sent home from school and he eventually had to withdraw them to the local public school. He could not keep up with his mortgage, and his house was repossessed. The last I heard of him was that he had moved back to his hometown. This was someone who had it all at some point. A very vibrant career and a bright future. But he had no Plan B for his career or financial future.

Another associate got laid off and by the very next month, he was soliciting loans from friends and family because his rent was due, and he had no money saved up. The threat of eviction hung over his head, adding unwanted panic to the pressure of trying to find a new job.

In another case, an executive in an organisation suffered a stroke and his career was unavoidably side-lined for a couple of years. During that time, he lost his job. His former employers moved on and his medical history made it difficult for him to get another job. He felt isolated, unappreciated and cheated. All the sleepless nights and immense time and energy poured into his job seemed to have all been for nothing. He was left saddled with a heavy financial burden that he could not carry. He recalled that one of the most painful points in that season was when his daughter graduated from university, but her certificate was withheld because of tuition fees owed.

And I could go on and on. There are simply too many cases like these to recount. But not all of them were dealing with the consequences of unexpected job loss. Some were trapped in jobs they hated. Day in, day out, they were stuck doing work they found unfulfilling and even soul-destroying, simply because they could not afford to lose the salary from the job.

Take Anthonia (not her real name) for example. She had been married for ten years without a child and endured heartaches, disappointments, as well as increasing pressure from the extended family in her bid to conceive. Finally, after numerous medical interventions supported by prayers, she was blessed with the fruit of the womb and gave birth to a baby boy. Then the conflict started.

She was working full-time and doing very well in her career when she had her child. When it came time to return to work after her maternity leave, the only thing uppermost on her mind was spending quality time with her child. She knew that if she returned to the work schedule that she maintained prior to having her baby, she would never get to spend time with him. He would still be sleeping when she left the house, and he would be fast asleep by the time she got back. She also deeply disdained the thought of outsourcing the care of the child she had spent ten years waiting for to hired help or even a family member. She deeply desired to raise her own child. But her family needed her income to sustain their lifestyle, so leaving her job was not a feasible option. She had no choice but to return to work.

But every time she left the child to go to the office, she became so depressed! She found it increasingly difficult to concentrate on the tasks at work because her mind was constantly at home with her child. And when she did have the rare opportunity to work from home, there were always gaps and lapses in the work produced by her team, which ended up creating more problems with her superiors. She was stuck going through the motions each day, as she desperately hoped and searched for a solution, any option, that would give her enough time to raise her child in the way she really wanted to and still have a career she could be proud of. Anthonia's desire for a balanced and financially rewarding career is valid. That is why I wrote this book; to show experts like her that there is a way out.

"Today, knowledge has power. It controls access to opportunities and advancement."
Peter Drucker

In case you are wondering why those three individuals called me the moment they received the news regarding their jobs, I believe they did for three reasons. Firstly, I own a Recruitment and Training company. They figured I could help them secure another job or train them to improve their chances of getting a new job. Secondly, they viewed me not just as a service provider but as a friend who was always pushing them about self-development and the need to have a plan B for their career.

Thirdly and probably most importantly, about two years before the layoff, all three of them had been present at a Personal Growth Strategy session I had spoken at. In that meeting, I had passionately challenged everyone present to take charge of their financial future and be intentional about acquiring transferable skills that could feed them and their families if they ever lost their jobs. They were made aware of the state of the economy and the job market. Again, this was pre-COVID. If it was bad then, it is calamitous now! They were told that hope was not a good strategy and merely hoping the future would take care of itself was a dangerous thing to do. I had even gone one step further by laying out clearly how they could leverage their expertise and secure their financial future by becoming a Trainer.

At the time, all three of them were excited about the prospect of multiplying their income and their impact by becoming a Trainer. They understood the implications of a sudden loss of income without a backup plan. Yet, for two years, they did nothing to take forward the advice I had given them. Even though they might not have had any control over whether they lost their jobs or not, they were certainly in control of the choice to proactively prepare for such unknown situations.

Later that night, as I reflected on the dilemma they now found themselves in, I wondered why my strong warnings had fallen on deaf ears. Then I realised that unfortunately, people seem to believe they are immune to such events as job loss, as if somehow it is a fate that belongs to other people out there. I have witnessed situations where individuals have refused to take responsibility for their own career until it was too late. I have seen this play out so many times and it is utterly perplexing!

This, of course, should not be the case, especially in the current Digital Age where many have made their fortunes and secured not just their financial future but of the generations to come by becoming thought leaders in their areas of expertise and sharing their knowledge with the world. The world has changed, irrevocably. COVID-19 has made sure of that! The traditional concept of "job security" is over. I suppose one good thing about the pandemic is that it has made it very clear how fragile the jobs market is. You cannot put your career entirely in the hands of an individual or organisation. You must create your own future! You must leverage your expertise by training others to do what comes easily to you.

> *"Failure is simply the opportunity to begin again, this time more intelligently."*
> Henry Ford

I was privileged to learn this lesson early on in my own professional career, when the threat of being sacked woke me up to the truth that "job security" is a very fragile concept indeed. A few years after I completed my first degree at university, I secured an entry level job to work in the Strategy and Business Process Improvement department of a new generation bank. One day during an induction program for new employees at the bank, the facilitator failed to show up. My unit was approached to help facilitate the training and since I was the most proficient person on the subject matter, Microsoft Excel, it was delegated to me. Fortunately for me, this was a subject I was not only proficient in, but extremely passionate about. This went some way in calming my nervousness at being suddenly thrust onto a stage without warning.

I stepped into that class and within a few minutes, the confidence from having expert knowledge of the subject kicked in and easily overrode my initial fear and hesitation. It was a huge success! I got 5-Star ratings from all the participants and it put me on the map as the go-to expert for Microsoft Excel at the bank.

Up until then, which was about four years into my professional career, no part of my work had given me as much personal fulfilment, recognition or joy as I had experienced during that four-hour training. And from that point on, I was hooked. I had always loved learning. To now be engaged in an activity that actually compelled me to learn more was just too incredible. Not only would I be impacting others by teaching them what I know, it was a mouth-watering opportunity to keep improving my knowledge and to become better and better at that skill. It was the perfect opportunity for me to fulfil my lifelong commitment to learning.

After that initial training session, I became restless because I wanted more. My job could barely hold my attention anymore. Somehow, I had lost interest in the business process improvement gig, which I loved at one point and assumed I would spend the rest of my career doing.

As time went on, I grew even more restless. I needed another shot at training. I went to meet a friend in the HR department to find out when the next induction would take place. It would not be for another two to three months, she said. I was gutted. I could not understand why it would take that long. Did the company not need people? I wanted so badly to experience that feeling of euphoria again.

About six weeks later, I was so excited when I was told the next class was starting and because my performance had been ranked higher than the person originally scheduled to deliver the training, I was now the preferred internal trainer for the Microsoft Excel course. I could barely sleep that weekend. I researched extensively and learned even more about the Microsoft Excel software. This was so amazing to me.

My session was scheduled for a Friday during the induction period. On Thursday afternoon, I reminded my boss that I had been asked to facilitate a session in the induction program the next day, and his response sent chills down my spine. "Young man, forget it!" He'd retorted angrily. "We have serious work to do here and I can't afford to spare you for some bullshit training program. The Human Resources (HR) department should source for their trainer somewhere else."

I could not believe it. What the heck was he talking about? I was so angry, I could not speak or concentrate on work for the rest of the day. I went to complain to the head of HR, and she told me that the internal training role was mandated by the CEO and that it was not a voluntary service. The CEO had already signed off on my name, so I was expected to be in class the next day. That was all I needed to hear. Knowing how uncooperative my boss could be, I decided not to say anything. I was certain if I did, he would have gone to the CEO to challenge HR's position and probably gotten his way.

The next day, I took off and went to class with some trepidation, knowing what I was doing could backfire and I could be in serious trouble later. I tried to reassure myself that I could not be sacked since I was following the CEO's instructions. This time, I was better prepared for the training and it went even better than the last one. About thirty minutes to the end of the session, one of my colleagues came into the training room and stood at the back. When he finally caught my eye, he made an ominous gesture by sliding his finger across his throat, indicating that I was a dead man, before quietly leaving the room. I knew I was in trouble.

My colleague was waiting for me the moment I stepped out of the class. "You are in big trouble! The boss has gone bunkers and is threatening to bring down the roof on you. I sincerely hope running this session was worth it. Bolaji, I am serious. He is unhinged!" He said with a smirk, clearly enjoying watching me squirm.

A part of me was afraid. Afraid of the possibility of getting fired. The other part was angry. Angry that my boss was being unreasonable. Why would he try to stop me from doing something that was mandated by the CEO? But I knew my boss well. I knew he would not care who gave the mandate, if it meant going against his explicit instruction to me. I could predict how he would react as soon as he laid his eyes on me. I knew that he would scream blue murder, throw an epic tantrum, and verbally abuse the living daylights out of me. I decided I would go on the offensive. If he shouted at me, I would shout back and match him decibel for decibel.

I entered the office and as soon as he saw me, as expected, he started screaming. And, I yelled back. My audacity must have completely taken him aback because he fell silent for about twenty seconds. When he regrouped, he was so enraged that he started coming towards me like he was going to strike me. The other members of the unit had to restrain him, and they pulled me out of the office so he could have the opportunity to calm down.

I went straight to HR department and asked to be transferred out of the unit, but my boss blocked it. I wanted to resign, but a couple of close associates spoke some sense into me and convinced me not to leave without getting another job.

I really do not know how I did not end up getting sacked that day. Yes, I was grateful that I still had a job and crucially, an income, but it was not a bed of roses from then on. I became trapped in a job I could no longer stand, working for a boss who now had it in for me! In that season, I experienced what it felt like to be stuck in a dead-end job that was slowly but surely sucking the life out of me. It was the exact push I needed, and it led me to begin taking intentional steps towards creating a future that would later turn out to be the most fulfilling and financially rewarding decision I have ever made.

"To hell with circumstances; I create opportunities."
Bruce Lee

From that day on, I knew very clearly in my mind that I wanted to create the future on my own terms. I knew that I wanted to build a training business and I went for it. I continued working hard at my job but squeezed time out during evenings and weekends to develop my interest in training. I researched extensively and developed my skills by grabbing every opportunity to deliver training programs, mostly without pay. What started as a small side project has today grown into a multi-million-dollar company.

The more I ventured into the Training industry, the more I discovered the immense demand for it. Training can never go out of demand. As long as people are trying to do something new, there will always be a need to teach them. As long as human beings are being recruited to work in organisations, there will always be a need to train them.

Take the COVID-19 pandemic for example. Lockdowns were enforced all over the world as schools, stores, offices and pretty much everything shut down. People were forced to live and work in a way that was completely new to them. Take schoolchildren as a case study. With schools shut, they had to get used to learning via online platforms such as Zoom, Microsoft Teams, Google hangout, etc. A significant number of them did not have prior knowledge or experience of the software. Although many parents were also working from home and some had a degree of proficiency in using Zoom, they were locked up in meetings all day and struggled to be home-school teacher and employee at the same time. One entrepreneur saw this as a golden opportunity to create an online course and teach people how to use Zoom. He created a step by step guide simple enough for a five-year old to understand. He marketed this course to private schools, and they welcomed it with open arms. Rather than have one teacher schedule a one-to-one Zoom training session with each of her thirty students or try to explain for the millionth time how to share a screen, her students were simply directed to complete the thirty-minute course and by the end of it they were good to go. Another example of the need for training during the pandemic is the significant rise in the demand for share trading courses as people looked to take advantage of fallen share prices. Yet another example is a smart entrepreneur who leveraged his deep knowledge of mergers and acquisition to create a course on how to buy companies that are distressed.

Whether you are a high earner who has survived the impact of COVID-19 and doing well to stay on top of your financial commitments, or you are struggling under a mountain of bills to pay due to sudden loss of income, the lesson I am hoping to pass across is this: your future is not guaranteed unless you create it. You cannot leave your future in the hands of people or organisations. You have to forge your own path. And what better way to do that than to leverage your knowledge and expertise? What better way to secure your financial future than by teaching others what you already know?

You may be thinking, "Yes, I hear you Bolaji. I agree with you, I need a backup plan. But my Plan B is to switch from a traditional industry like Banking to a more promising one like Tech." (Or, insert whatever fits your unique situation.) Whilst that could be a good idea, the unfortunate truth is, changing careers is hard. Very hard. It took a lot of time, effort, and resources to get to your current level of proficiency, success and income in your career. You have acquired a wealth of skills, capabilities and experience that make it easy for you to succeed at your job. Succeeding in a new career will not require any less! In the first few years, you can expect a loss of momentum as well as a steep learning curve. It will require a great deal of time, energy, and other resources to replicate your success in the new career. Sadly, people typically underestimate the cost of success in a new venture but overestimate the benefits they stand to gain. Hence, nine out of ten new initiatives fail.

Instead of starting all over again, a more realistic and proximate approach is to leverage your current expertise by creating and delivering in-person or online training programs. This is one of the most powerful and rewarding career shifts you can make, since you already possess the necessary ingredients for success. The wealth of knowledge, skills and experience you have gathered over the years can be refined and organised into a goldmine of training opportunities through which you can build a successful career or simply fortify your finances by creating an additional stream of income.

And it is never too late to start. Those three people who reached out to me that day did so because they knew there was still a way out. And thankfully, they were now ready to take action on the advice that I had given them two years earlier. By the end of my meeting with the last of the three that day, I made up my mind to develop a solution targeted at helping experts significantly reduce their vulnerability and the impact of job loss on them and their families. Nobody should have to go through what they were going through.

So, I got to work and created a pragmatic blueprint that experts can easily implement to leverage their expertise and generate additional or alternative income as a Trainer. Over the next three months I worked with those three individuals to turn their fortunes around and start earning money through training. Two of them are now working as full-time trainers doing very well. The third one was hired full time by one of the organisations he had trained for during his freelance stint. In a very short time, I helped them turn their desperate situations into successful outcomes. If they can do it, so can you. This book details exactly how.

> *The wealth of knowledge, skills and experience you have gathered over the years can be refined and organised into a goldmine of training opportunities through which you can build a successful career or simply fortify your finances by creating an additional stream of income.*

KEY TAKEAWAYS

- "Job security" is a very fragile concept. No one is immune to losing their job, no matter how highly proficient, experienced or remunerated they are in that job.

- The feelings of frustration you may experience from being trapped in a dead-end job or unfulfilling career is an excellent opportunity to create change.

- But changing careers is hard. It will require a tremendous amount of time, energy and money to build your career back up to where you left off. Most people do not have that luxury.

- The most efficient and truly rewarding way to invigorate your career and multiply your income is to leverage your experience and expertise in your current field as a Trainer. This allows you to build upwards from where you are without having to start afresh.

- The COVID-19 pandemic has created an irreversible demand for digital training. Even in these hard times, you can make money and impact lives as a Trainer.

3

YOU TOO CAN AND MUST BECOME A TRAINER

"I have come to believe that a great teacher is a great artist and that there are as few as there are any other great artists. Teaching might even be the greatest of the arts since the medium is the human mind and spirit."
John Steinbeck

Michael (not his real name) was a senior business executive who was spending ungodly hours at a job that, other than the salary he was earning, he could not care less about anymore. His children were growing up so fast that soon enough, they would be out of the house and he would have missed out on his best years as a parent. He was physically and emotionally burnt out, and his doctor had already issued him with several stern warnings about the health problems that awaited him if he did not start taking better care of himself. But with him working sixteen to eighteen-hour days, no matter how hard he tried to prioritise his health, no fitness plan lasted more than a couple of weeks.

Every day, as he made his way to work before the crack of dawn, he fantasised about living a better life. He wished with every fibre of his being that he could do something more fulfilling, more worthwhile with his career. But he also knew that he could not just walk away from the income the job provided.

When Michael reached out to me for advice, he had expected me to recommend companies and jobs that would fit his criteria for a dream job. I wasted no time in telling him that such an opportunity exists, and it would be just right for him. I told him that because he was an extremely competent professional with years of experience in a high-demand industry, there was a superbly rewarding career opportunity that would enable him to continue earning a sustainable income, have more time to spend with his family, and impact more lives than he had ever done as a business executive.

His excitement was palpable. He simply could not believe what he was hearing. I had just told him that his deepest desires were not only possible, but well within his grasp. He urged me to link him with that job opportunity straightaway so that he could begin working towards it.

So, I looked him squarely in the face and said, "You should become a Trainer." It was as if I had poured a bucket of cold water on him. His face fell and the first words out of his mouth were, "Trainer? Common, Bolaji, be serious. How can I make the kind of money I make now training people?"

I laughed at that statement and pointed at myself as if to say, I am living proof that it is possible. He considered that truth for a moment and then conceded. "Yes, well, I know you've built an incredibly successful company as a Trainer. But I'm not you. Not everyone can stand in front of people and talk for a living. I have a paralysing fear of public speaking!"

I had heard that excuse countless times. So, rather than argue with him, I decided to use the shock tactic. "I bet you're nowhere near as scared of standing in front of people as I am." It worked. He stared at me in disbelief. "Really? But you always appear so confident in all the presentations I've seen you deliver, so sure of yourself!" He exclaimed.

"Yes, that may be true, but it certainly didn't come automatically to me. I worked hard at it. Public speaking is a skill and like any other, can and should be mastered by everyone. Do you know that till today, I still feel nervous every time I step out to speak to a group of people?"

"Wow," he laughed. "I definitely didn't see that coming. So, you're saying like you, I also can leverage and monetise all the expertise I've gained over the years by becoming a Trainer? Even if I don't have any prior training experience other than leading team meetings?"

"Absolutely! Anyone can become a Trainer."

I wish I could say the conversation ended there. But he still had many questions that kept popping up in his mind to challenge the idea that he could build a successful career as a Trainer. And I was excited to answer them. We continued the conversation over a couple of weeks until he was fully convinced that he could build a successful career as a Trainer and coach.

"Teaching is the profession that teaches all the other professions."
Unknown

I have paraphrased and addressed the main questions he and others like him have asked me below, so that you too can come to a place where you are absolutely convinced you can make money and multiply your impact by transferring your knowledge to others and helping them gain proficiency. I believe every subject matter expert can and should become a Trainer. And because you are reading this book, you have demonstrated a willingness to know how to leverage your expertise to secure your financial future. In fact, I will go a step further and say, "You must become a Trainer."

But I'm not renowned or influential enough to be considered an expert

One of the most prevalent reasons people do not step out and do something they are very capable of doing is what is called the "imposter syndrome." That is, someone who has years of experience and has become a leader in their field still doubts their accomplishments and feels like a fraud waiting to be exposed. No matter how high they rise, they still think, "I am not an expert." The truth is, the whole world does not need to know you for you to be an expert. If you have mastered any knowledge, skill or experience enough to consistently produce results with it, then you are regarded as an expert in that area and can therefore teach others to do the same.

If you know your subject area well, all you need to do is learn how to create a successful training program out of what you know. And that is what this book is all about. Once that foundational knowledge is in place, the rest is simply being willing to take consistent action as you build your training profession over time. As long as you have in-depth knowledge of your subject matter, and the relevant experience and education to back it up, you can become a successful trainer online or offline.

But I have multiple areas of interest and expertise, how do I pick one?

If you have gained expertise in different areas over the years, it can be daunting trying to narrow them down and settle on the one that will work well for you as a Trainer. That is why one of the most valuable parts of this book is the chapter I dedicated to helping you pick your niche or area of specialty. It is well structured, detailed and has exercises and tools that will help you move from being a generalist to a specialist. A lot of people suffer from shiny object syndrome, where they follow after every new trend and end up chasing too many things. The critical thing, especially at the beginning of any venture is to choose a particular area and focus on it. Later in this book, we will look at this in depth.

But I hate promoting myself, how will I make money as a Trainer?

This is a huge problem for most people. I have seen highly skilled people who will not hesitate to convene meetings and deliver trainings within their workplace or social groups. As long as there is no direct exchange of money, they are extremely comfortable gathering people together. They volunteer to train people at church or at work, friends and family or even strangers for free. But once the idea of charging a fee outside of a structured salaried environment comes up, they become petrified. They are afraid of being rejected and hearing "No", or having their reputation tainted by people labelling them as a money-grabbing "salesperson". This fear is so real to them that it stops them from stepping out to secure paying clients.

Yes, I understand how crippling the fear of rejection can be. Nobody enjoys failing or being rejected. That is why I have dedicated a chapter in this book to marketing. I teach you how to ease into sales and marketing by building your business connections gradually from the known (and comfortable) to the unknown. I teach you how to leverage your network in a non-aggressive way to build your training portfolio.

Everybody knows somebody, whether it is friends, family, or colleagues at work. Start from there. And then, you must go all out to deliver value. You must do such an outstanding job that people will be excited to refer you to others without you having to push too hard. It would no longer be friends and family half-heartedly promoting your service out of pity or concern, but because they genuinely believe in what you are doing. As the referrals start to roll in, you can begin to gradually build a list of potential clients.

That is precisely how I got my training business off the ground. When I started the company, we organised a two-day program and sent out invitations for a free capacity-building training to fifty companies we wanted to partner with. About twenty-two accepted our invitation and showed up. For a new start up that was relatively unknown, this was a high rate of success. But it was not a lucky break. I had invested a lot of time into researching the biggest needs of those organisations, as well as the best program that would meet those needs. I also ensured the benefits were communicated clearly and passionately.

Then, crucially, because we delivered the program so well, we received glowing testimonials from those reputable organisations that we subsequently used to promote our programs. Nobody asked whether those were paying clients or not. All that mattered was, we had credible professional experience that made it easy for other companies to do business with us. And of course, some of those twenty-two companies went on to become our clients. The most important thing is to find a way to actually bring people to the table, whether paid or free. And once you have that opportunity to train people, you must do it excellently, so that the people keep coming back.

But training is capital intensive – for example, you have to hire an expensive venue, and I don't have that kind of funds

It is no longer necessary to have a physical location to deliver trainings. During the COVID-19 era, we have seen events take place online that we would never have imagined possible. Online weddings, birthday parties, theatre performances, and the like have become the norm. The pandemic has successfully changed the way we work, live, and engage with the people in our communities. And the general consensus is that things will never return to the way they used to be.

Technology has made it so easy nowadays to teach people located over the world from the comfort of your living room. You do not actually have to physically meet up with people anymore. And even if you do, you would not have to hire an expensive meeting space to begin with. When I started as a Trainer, I had situations where I ran my one-on-one training sessions in hotel lobbies, and all I needed to do was pay for drinks. And there were also times when a company had a venue we wanted to use, and we offered to train their staff in exchange for the free use of their facilities.

At another time, whilst still working as an employee, I asked my boss for permission to use my office during the weekend to run Microsoft Excel trainings and he agreed on the condition that I would open the training up to other members of his team. So, it is no longer the case that you must spend huge amounts of money to deliver a training session. There are different ways to go about it. You can find many creative ways that will fit within your budget easily. I did not start with a penny. I just started with what I knew, my drive, and my passion and I was able to do a lot. The most important requirement for becoming a Trainer is your know-how and drive for success, not money. If you have the know-how and the drive, the channel you will use to train people can be easily figured out, you just need to be creative about it and you will do well.

But I'm too busy to build a new career or business

It depends on how badly you want to secure your financial future, and how important it is to you to impact lives. Most people spend the best part of their lives being comfortable in their discomfort. Someone described this scenario as "Acceptable Underperformance". They are dissatisfied with their situation and desire change, but they never do anything about it. And after some time, they learn to live with their dissatisfaction. Do not be one of those people. Think of the benefits, think of why you are doing it, think of the impact you can have on yourself and other people, think of the value you can create. That should motivate you enough to create the time for it.

Most people spend the best part of their lives being comfortable in their discomfort.

Another way to overcome the issue of lack of time is to carefully observe how you are spending your time. Tighten up your use of time. Nobody is so busy that they cannot find at least an hour or two daily to invest in a side project. When I started my business, I had not resigned from my nine to five. I was still working full time. During the week, I focused entirely on work, but dedicated all my weekends to finding people whose needs I could meet. It was almost as if I walked around carrying a banner, asking for who wanted to be trained, because that was something I was determined to deepen my capabilities in.

I tried as much as possible to use my commute time as an opportunity to learn something new or even to create content. I used my phone to record myself teaching and then transferred the content to paper when I got home. Sometimes, I invested the time I would have spent in leisure activities such as watching football, into building my business. Most times when I am on holiday, my days are divided into two parts – one part for relaxation and fun, and the other for learning something interesting that will contribute directly or indirectly to my work. It is all about prioritisation. Keep the reasons you are doing it firmly before you as a source of motivation and arrange your time to make your training profession a priority. If it is important to you, you will find the time for it.

But I have a crippling fear of public speaking

Coincidentally, this was also my biggest fear. The truth is, I am naturally a shy person. In fact, I am extremely shy. But I made a decision early on that I would not allow that stop me from achieving my goals and aspirations. I started reading a lot about public speaking. One funny advice I got that actually worked for me was, before getting up on any stage to speak, imagine that everyone in the audience owes you money. If someone owes you money, there is a certain audacity with which you would speak to them. In the same way, just hold that image of your audience as people who owe you money and you will find confidence and boldness rising from within you.

Another important truth you must accept is, fear of public speaking is rooted in self-centredness. The reason you are afraid is, you have made it all about you; how people will judge you or not celebrate you, or how you would feel if you messed up. The more you focus on yourself, the more scared you will become. But it is not about you at all. Do not focus on yourself.

Another important truth you must accept is, fear of public speaking is rooted in self-centredness. The reason you are afraid is, you have made it all about you; how people will judge you or not celebrate you, or how you would feel if you messed up.

As a Trainer, what should drive you is your love for helping people by sharing what you know. When you stand in front of an audience, your primary concern should be how you can help them, how you can add value to them. See them as people who made a sacrifice to come there to listen to you, not to massage your ego but because they have needs you can meet. Take your attention off yourself and put it on them. Look at the audience with empathy and compassion and know that you are there for them; not for yourself. If you approach your training with that mindset, before you know it, you would have forgotten about your fear because you are more focused on doing your best to meet those needs. The program will go so well that you will wonder why you were even afraid in the first place. That is the secret to public speaking – understanding that it is not about you, it is about your audience. Till tomorrow, I am still afraid of public speaking, but I rise up each time and do it well because I know it is not about me.

Lastly, start small and build up gradually. Nobody gets good at anything without practice and repetition. You can even start by doing it on a part-time basis. I know a couple of people who started off by teaching in their churches or amongst their colleagues. Some joined professional public speaking groups like Toastmasters to gain experience. Consistent practice will accelerate your growth. The sooner you start, the better.

But with so much information out there, how will I keep my knowledge-base up to date?

To be a Trainer, you must have the mindset of a student. You cannot give what you do not have, right? To be successful as a Trainer, you need to be really, *really* good at learning. You must be a lifelong learner. There is no way around it. Training is a seamless flow of learning and teaching. The more you learn, the more effective you will be at training others. And the more you train others, the more you learn. They reinforce each other. Becoming a Trainer forced me to learn as much as I could so that I could add value to my clients. And that process of learning ended up enriching my own life so much that it opened the door to more opportunities. I began to see more and more ways that I could create value for myself and for my clients.

In his book, Seven Habits of Highly Effective People, Stephen Covey said the moment you learn something new, try to teach it to someone within a day or two because the best way to retain what you learn is by teaching it. Based on that principle alone, anything I want to be very good at, I learn it and quickly teach it so that I can become better at it. Teaching it leads me to the point where I know it so well that it becomes a business opportunity bearing great rewards. Learning and teaching are inseparable. It is a chain reaction that keeps reinforcing itself in a never-ending cycle.

How I built a multi-million Training business from the ground up

Now, I can hardly be credible if I am encouraging you to take a step that I have not yet taken myself. The reason I can be so bold when I say that anyone can become a successful Trainer is because I have lived it. I did not have my training company handed to me. I built it from the ground up.

In the previous chapter, I shared with you how I stumbled into the training profession. As a young professional, I was asked to deliver a Microsoft Excel training to new employees when the scheduled Trainer failed to turn up. I also shared how my newfound love for training was almost immediately crushed by my boss who was strongly against me delivering that training.

After that explosive episode with my boss, I had to take a step back with respect to facilitating any more programs until the whole thing blew over. But as luck would have it, a couple of months later, he was promoted into a much bigger role to lead another division. The person who took over the unit was more accommodating of my passion for training. This made it a lot easier to continue pursuing training opportunities within the organisation. However, I was restricted to teaching the Microsoft Excel course and because the company was slowing down on its recruitment drive, the opportunities for me to train were few and far in-between.

So, I started looking for external opportunities. The first one I found was volunteering for an NGO to train kids and prepare them for life ahead. Next, a couple of professional friends discovered how good I was with the Microsoft Excel software and asked me to train them on the weekends. And they actually paid me for it. I found it very interesting that people were willing to pay me for something I would have done for free. Up until that point, my focus had not really been on getting paid. Of course, with entrepreneurial blood running through my veins, the moment I got paid I was awakened to the possibility of making a business out of it. I began to research how I could become a full time Trainer. I started reading books and one of the books I read suggested that I should start off by working for a company that specialised in the business I wanted to set up. That way, I could gather valuable experience and build strong alliances and relationships within that industry. This would then give me a huge advantage when the time came to launch my own business. So, I doubled up my search for such a job.

While searching, I received a job offer from a reputable organisation that wanted me to head their process improvement unit and I turned it down. The reason was simple. I was absolutely clear in my mind what direction I wanted to move in and after exploring all possible options, I knew that the job would not take me towards my goal of becoming a full time Trainer. Even though it was a fantastic opportunity, it was an easy decision for me to let it go.

Then one day, I was speaking to a friend who worked in the HR department about my desire to become a Trainer and she told me about a boutique recruitment and training firm that was looking for somebody to head their recruitment business. At the time, I was not interested in recruitment, even though I could do it. At first, I was going to turn it down but when I thought about it deeper, I decided that since training was also a major part of their business, I would still be in that space. It was more proximate to my ultimate objective than where I was at the time. Besides, I was bored out my mind working in my job.

I called the key person in the company to have a chat and it went so well, I was invited to visit their offices. By the end of that visit, I was hooked. I saw that training was a fundamental part of their business, with a couple of designated training rooms, and more importantly, I was assured that there would be more than enough opportunities to train and to learn the business.

I took a pay cut to join that company because I could see how it would bring me closer to my goal of establishing a training business. It turned out to be a fantastic experience and one of the best decisions I have ever made. I was exposed to not only training as a vocation but to the business side of training as well. I quickly learned that there was a difference between training as a vocation and training as a business, which later proved to be an extremely valuable experience for me when I started my business.

While there, I learned that there is a massive difference between training friends or colleagues for free and training professionals or delegates who are paying you for your service. When I trained new employees at my old job, or friends at the weekend, the stakes were not very high. But now, I was training people whose companies had paid large sums of money and therefore, had very high expectations. I remember running a program for a client that did not go well and it knocked my confidence. I was also getting frustrated by the fact that I did not seem able to sustain an excellent standard in all my training sessions. Sometimes my sessions were outstanding, sometimes they were just okay and at other times they fell completely flat. What exactly was the issue? Why was I struggling to deliver a consistently outstanding experience for my clients?

To find the answer, I started reading, studying and researching. I knew that the lack of consistency could not simply be excused away or left to chance. During my search, I discovered that training is both an art and a science. And to be successful at it, you must be able to design your participants' learning for maximum impact. That was when I decided to get trained to become a professional Trainer. It was no longer enough that I was passionate about training, I had to become highly skilled at it too. I signed up for Train the Trainer programs and I engaged coaches and mentors I could learn from.

This cycle of learning and improving my training skills continued throughout my time at that company until I left to start my own business. Incidentally, when I started my business, it was a lot easier to get the recruitment part of the business off the ground, so that was what I focused on to start with. The training business came later after we were able to overcome the biggest objection we faced when we started offering training programs. The objection was simple; we were a new company and potential clients wanted proof we could deliver what we promised. They wanted references from clients we had trained. Although I had a wealth of experience at my old training job, I could not cite it because I had been training on behalf of the organisation. They wanted something that was directly associated with my company's brand. That was a bit of a problem and we struggled initially.

During my search, I discovered that training is both an art and a science.

Again, I started looking for a solution through books and courses. I attended a course where I asked the facilitator for ideas on how to overcome the lack of suitable experience. He gave me a strategy that turned out to be one of the best things that could have happened to my business at that time.

He asked us to research a topic that would be extremely valuable to the clients we were targeting, that would deliver quick and measurable results for them. And then, to organise a training program for them free of charge. That would help my company gather the much-needed training experience. We got to work straightaway. We surveyed those clients and asked about the biggest challenges they were facing. I leveraged my networks and found out that the biggest headache they had was developing and executing an effective business strategy. Once we were clear about what they needed the most, we developed training programs to meet those needs.

We put together the most effective business strategy program possible. It took us over two months to design a two-day program. We made sure that every aspect of the program including lunch and tea breaks were designed for maximum impact. Then, we sent invitations to fifty organisations to attend our program free of charge.

A couple of them wanted to know why it was free and we were honest with them. It was free because we were trying to break into the market, but we were also confident we had incredible value to offer. Almost half of the companies we invited turned up for the program and we delivered an exceptional training. All the performance ratings were between four and five stars. We got the participants to complete feedback forms and six people took up our offer to record testimonial videos. We also made sure that every delegate left with a beautifully designed brochure promoting our training programs.

Three months after the program, we were working with at least eight of the companies and we just grew from there. Within five years, we were making about a million dollars per year in revenue, just from the training side of the business. By this time, we had realised that the people who influenced and made the key training decisions in an organisation were the HR and Learning & Development departments. So, we dug deep and became specialists in training HR and L&D professionals.

The first of such trainings that we created was Competency-Based Learning and Development. A delegate from one of the biggest organisations in the country attended the program and she was so impressed that she invited us to speak at her company's HR strategy retreat. This eventually led to one of our biggest projects at the time. We were commissioned to conceptualise, design and implement a program worth almost half a million dollars to the company. This was the opportunity that really established us in the training business and the business simply grew exponentially after that.

Throughout this book I will share with you the same insights and strategies that helped me achieve this level of success as a Trainer. And I am certain they will help you too. As you read on, my biggest advice to you is this; do not sit on your gold mine of expertise, hoping the future will take care of itself. Start long before you need to start. Let me repeat that: start long before you need to start. Do not wait until career curve balls are thrown at you and you are mandated to create change. Start when the stakes are not so high. This will give you a huge advantage and the opportunity to build up the necessary momentum. The earlier you start building a financially secure future by becoming a Trainer, the better for you, your family and the people you are called to serve.

> *...do not sit on your gold mine of expertise, hoping the future will take care of itself. Start long before you need to start.*

KEY TAKEAWAYS

- Every expert can, and should, become a Trainer. There is no better way to multiply your impact, your income, and your expertise all at the same time.

- Many experts struggle with fears and doubts that are preventing them from leveraging their expertise to become Trainers, when in fact, most of these fears are baseless. They are sitting on a gold mine of experience, skills and knowledge that, if used in the service of others, is guaranteed to bring them more influence, impact and income.

- You can easily rid yourself of "Imposter syndrome," fear of rejection, fear of public speaking, fear of failure, or any other terrorising feeling that has been preventing you from stepping out by studying and implementing the insights and strategies shared throughout this book.

- There is no better time to start securing your financial future than right now. Start when the stakes are not so high. Do not wait until life throws curve balls at you and you are forced to create change under duress.

- You do not need a huge amount of money, time or popularity to get started as a Trainer. My own journey to building a multi-million-dollar training business started with training friends, working during evenings and weekends, and hosting training sessions in hotel lobbies. The most important requirement for becoming a trainer is your expertise and an unwavering drive for success.

4

12 COMPELLING REASONS WHY YOU MUST BECOME A TRAINER

"A good teacher is like a candle – it consumes itself to light the way for others."
Mustafa Kemal Atatürk

Eyiwa (not his real name) was a C-Level Executive in a medium-size tech company when he and his wife decided to relocate their family to Canada. They were particular about giving their four children the best education possible, and they believed the relocation would make it possible for them to do so. But moving to Canada and starting afresh also meant that Eyiwa had to sacrifice seniority and pay grade in his career. He went from being a Senior Marketing Officer to working as an IT support assistant in a small pharmaceutical company in Canada.

Furthermore, his wife could not work. Taking care of three children without help (childcare was not an affordable option) made it almost impossible for her to follow her well-laid plans for career progression. Although she had been a fast-rising HR professional, the situation had compelled her to become a stay-at-home mum without an income. The family now had to rely on a significantly lower income than they were used to.

Three years on and the situation was still pretty much the same, if not worse, and Eyiwa had grown increasingly frustrated with the lack of progress in his career and the impact it was having on their quality of life. The family was in a dire situation financially that neither of them had seen coming. Most of the assumptions they had made before the move came crashing down and their dream of creating a financially secure life was proving a lot more complicated than they had imagined.

The solution that got them out of their dilemma was very simple. Although Eyiwa and his wife were constrained by the limitations of their physical environment – securing high paying jobs in Canada was a mid to long term plan, they soon discovered that modern technology had presented them with limitless possibilities. Eyiwa for starters, had over fifteen years of highly successful marketing and brand management experience. He was a marketing expert.

With his level of expertise, he discovered that he could be of service to small businesses who needed help in driving their sales through effective marketing. And he could make money to boost his family's income in the process! So, he got to work. He invested his evenings and weekends into creating an online course. He reached out to his networks back in Africa and within six months, he was making a decent side income working with businesses in Africa from his home in Canada.

By becoming a trainer, Eyiwa had successfully achieved three phenomenal outcomes. One, he was able to maintain his working knowledge of marketing – an in-demand industry – and keep abreast of new developments, models, and trends in that career. Two, he was able to generate a sustainable income for his family and three, he was able to do it flexibly, whilst working full time at his day job.

"A teacher affects eternity: he can never tell where his influence stops."
Henry Adams

12 Compelling Reasons Why You Must Become a Trainer

One of the most difficult decisions that people have to make in life is their choice of career or business. People ask me all the time, "What is the best career or business idea for me to pursue?" There is no easy answer to this question because there are many factors to be considered and what is often perceived as the "best" choice is relative.

Having said that, if the principle of leverage is applied when choosing a professional pathway, then I can confidently recommend a career or business as a Trainer to anyone seeking an answer to this question.

The Oxford dictionary defines leverage as a means of maximising advantage. If we apply leverage to career or business, becoming a Trainer offers one of the biggest, yet most underrated methods of optimising the advantages available to smart and self-driven individuals.

Becoming a Trainer has the potential to multiply your efforts and create compelling benefits in several areas. Here, I highlight twelve compelling reasons why you should seriously consider a career or business in training.

Reason #1
Multiple Streams of Income

A five-year study on the habits of millionaires was carried out by Tom Corley, the author of "Rich Habits" and one of the major distinguishing factors between the rich and the poor was the number of streams of income possessed by each group. He found that self-made millionaires usually had more than one stream of income, while those who were barely surviving and living from paycheque to paycheque often only depended on one income. According to his study, 65% of self-made millionaires had at least three streams of income; 45% of self-made millionaires had at least four streams of income, and 29 % of self-made millionaires had five or more streams of income.

In this economy, creating multiple streams of income is no longer a luxury; it is a necessity. If you want to survive these uncertain times, you must diversify your income portfolio. Unfortunately, for most people, their only source of income is their salary. But surely, high unemployment rates and job losses in this COVID-era is presenting us with mounting evidence that nobody's job is safe. It is simply too risky to depend only on your job for all your income. Warren Buffet, the investment mogul, said, "Never depend on a single income. Make investments to create a second source."

Imagine a bathtub with multiple outlets in it and with water pouring into it through a single tap. It is practically impossible to keep water in such a tub. This describes the financial condition of most people. They have only one source of income but many expenses. Naturally, they are barely able to get by. And they usually do not have residual income for rainy days.

FIGURE 1: The Bathtub Scenario

Now, imagine if the same bathtub had two or three extra taps pouring water into it and all the holes causing unnecessary leakage were blocked. What would happen? Not only would you be able to retain your income, but you would also have a fall-back plan for eventualities.

FIGURE 1b: The Bathtub Scenario B

Building a career or starting a business as a Trainer opens multiple "taps" to boost your earning potential. Whether you choose to build a training business, create online courses, or train within an organisation, becoming a Trainer offers you immense opportunities to create an additional income stream. This income diversification puts less pressure on your finances and helps you to take advantage of new opportunities.

Reason #2
Greater Effectiveness in Area of Expertise

"Intellectual growth should commence at birth and cease only at death."
Albert Einstein

One reason I believe practically everyone should be a Trainer is that it offers you the added benefit of continuous learning and competency development. The more opportunities you have to teach someone a skill in your area of expertise, the better you also will become in executing that skill.

The great Philosopher Seneca said: "While we teach, we learn." This is known as the Protégé Effect and is based on the idea that, when you teach a material or topic to others, it reinforces your own understanding. This phenomenon has been shown to be true by several studies and it works because of a number of reasons[3]. One, teaching a topic forces you to think critically on it. For your students to understand what you are saying and not leave them confused, you have to be able to distil the information into clear and coherent thoughts. Two, by teaching that topic, you are exposing yourself to different perspectives and can therefore give your students a multidimensional learning experience. Three, fear of failure will motivate you to actually put the required effort into your preparation. How would you be able to teach something you have not understood

While we teach, we learn.

---
[3] Medium.com

49

yourself? Four, the questions asked by the students and the demand they make on your knowledge in their quest to understand the content is guaranteed to open up new perspectives regarding the subject matter and further enrich and deepen your knowledge in that area. And lastly, teaching exposes you to a wide range of tools and techniques as you seek to improve your delivery and find the best way to engage your students.

Competency is defined as the knowledge, skill, and attitude required to do something well. There are five different competency levels attainable in any career or business. At Level 1, you are considered a novice. You know little or nothing about your subject area. Then, you progress to Level 2: *Can do it with help*. On this level, you need supervision.

At Level 3, you can do it without help. Here, you have attained a level of competency that allows you to produce and deliver results on your own. This is a very important but hazardous level because, unfortunately, this is where most people stop and peak in their career or business. At this level, they become static and start to decline. This is where people claim to have gained ten years of experience, which is really one year of experience repeated nine times.

Level 4 is to teach others. This is so critical to career and business success because the demand placed on the teacher by the student forces him to dig deeper and learn more. Again, people tend to stop here and miss the chance to truly gain mastery in their careers.

At Level 5, you redefine the way things are done. This

is where true success and unimaginable rewards lie. This is where people innovate and radically change industries, redefine market boundaries, and disrupt institutions that are slow or unwilling to change. Becoming a Trainer is a guaranteed way to rise through the levels of competency at an accelerated rate.

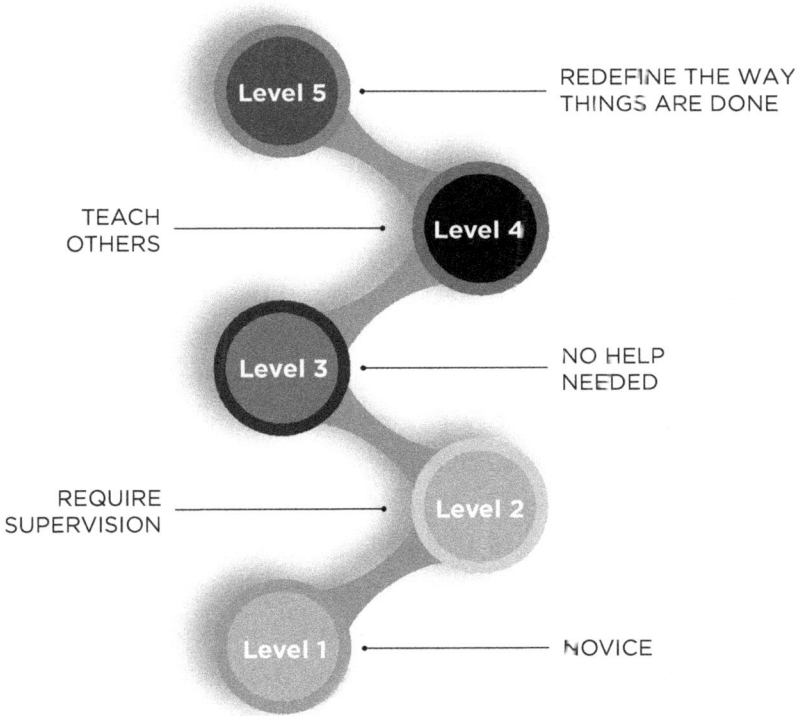

FIGURE 2: 5 Competence Level Framework

Reason #3
Exposure to New and Bigger Opportunities

When you are a Trainer and you are very good at what you do, doors of opportunities beyond what you could possibly imagine will open up to you. This is because you will benefit from the all-or-nothing rule which states that, "If you do one thing well, people assume that you do everything well."

In the 1980s, Robert Ronstadt carried out a twelve-year study into the subsequent career and business success of a cohort of MBA graduates. He found that those who created multiple business ventures using what he called the "Corridor Principle" turned out be the most successful. According to him, "The Corridor Principle states that the mere act of starting a venture enables entrepreneurs to see other venture opportunities they could neither see nor take advantage of until they had started their initial venture.4" In order words, action creates insights that lead to further action. This has proven to be true time and time again in the training profession. Training has an immense potential to open doors to many more opportunities that would not have been possible without your exposure and visibility as a Trainer. For example, it is very possible to transition from a Trainer to becoming a coach, consultant, or advisor for organisations.

In order words, action creates insights that lead to further action.

---

4 Ronstadt, R. (1988) 'The Corridor Principle', Journal of Business Venturing, 3(1), pp. 31-40.

Reason #4
Wealth Creation While You Sleep

One of the fastest and most profitable ways of getting your expertise out into the global marketplace is by creating online courses. As a Trainer, you have the opportunity to take advantage of the growth of this rapidly expanding market by productising your know-how and teaching it virtually to thousands of people all over the world. You can literally make money while you sleep.

Intellectual entrepreneurship is not just the new in-thing; it is the fastest way to become a successful entrepreneur. Rather than having a speculative business idea that may or may not pan out, why not go down the route of setting up a highly proven, scalable, and profitable business model built or your intellectual property? This is one of the most rewarding things you can do to create the kind of impact, income and freedom you desire.

Reason #5
Strategic Connections and Networks

One undeniable fact of life is, the answers, money, access, power, and influence you need to get what you want in this world lie in the hands of people. To achieve any goal, you need people to help you do it. Without a vast network, your success will be capped. A deep, strong network is a necessity for a successful life. Everything you accomplish in life will happen through people, a team, or a strong network.

As a Trainer, you have the unique opportunity to connect with a lot of interesting people that could prove valuable to your training career or business. The fact that your participants are investing in your training is an indication of their aspiration for personal growth and success. And because you are helping them learn, grow, and develop, it puts you at an advantage to benefit from them. It gives you the platform through which you can connect with them and form good, highly productive relationships.

Your competence is the best basis for developing strategic alliances. Many good trainers have come into new and unanticipated opportunities such as job offers, new training or consulting briefs after delivering a training session. Your role as a Trainer will bring many people across your path. These connections might prove pivotal to your future success if you know how to leverage and take full advantage of them.

Reason #6
Continuous Personal Development and Growth

"Learn as if you were not reaching your goal and as though you were scared of missing it."
Confucius

It was Eli Cohen who said, **"Without continuous personal development, you are all that you will ever become, and hell starts when the person you are meets the person you could have been."** Investing in personal development is one of the most important things anyone can do to guarantee a productive and fulfilling life.

Personal development is the process of understanding and developing yourself to achieve your fullest potential. It is a vital part of a person's growth, maturity, success, and fulfilment. It is the foundation for a mature personality, better relationships, happiness, success, and prosperity. Unfortunately, because personal development is neither taught as a subject in schools, nor is it required as a certifiable skill for employment, most people ignore it entirely to their detriment.

As a Trainer, you will be forced to engage in continuous personal development because you will realise one fundamental truth – **you cannot give what you do not have**. To excel in your role, you will naturally have to invest in yourself and, as a result, continuously transform your own life.

Reason #7
Knowledge Capital

"For the best return on your money, pour your purse into your head."
Benjamin Franklin

As far as personal assets are concerned, knowledge is the most valuable asset you can own. And unlike other assets that diminish in value with time and use, knowledge actually and unavoidably increases in value with constant use. This makes knowledge a vital asset, which anyone can cultivate and own. Benjamin Franklin said, "An investment in knowledge always pays the best interest."

The saying that knowledge is power is not absolutely true. Knowledge applied to the right purpose is what constitutes power. As a Trainer, you will be required to apply and share what you know, which is the source of power that can be leveraged to accomplish many benefits, including income generation, strong networks, new job opportunities, and personal growth.

...you cannot give what you do not have.

Reason #8
Starting Your Own Business

If you are considered an expert in your field, you can easily leverage the same skill and expertise to start your own training business. As a Trainer, one of the benefits of starting your own business is that start-up costs are meagre. You already have the knowledge, expertise, and the right connections. All you need is a plan and the right sales and marketing strategy that will position you appropriately before your clients.

Becoming a Trainer is a clear and viable path to owning your own business. It is arguably the most scalable, predictable and repeatable business model out there today. Several experts have successfully created massive impact by leveraging their expertise to start and own a profitable information business. You too can do the same. And there is no better time to start your own training business than right now.

Reason #9
Personal Fulfilment and Satisfaction

"Our greatest personal fulfilment comes when we contribute to improving the welfare of others."
Gail Lynne Godwin

Not every career is fulfilling. The inner fulfilment and satisfaction that come from helping others grow, improve, and succeed are beyond quantifiable. This is what successful Trainers do. They consistently share impactful knowledge that adds value to their audience and helps them become better individuals. Nothing brings a person more joy than becoming an instrument of another person's transformation.

You will definitely be rewarded financially as a Trainer. But beyond the financial gains is the fulfilment of seeing people you have taught succeed because of what they learnt from you. Money cannot buy this kind of reward.

Nothing brings a person more joy than becoming an instrument of another person's transformation.

Reason #10
Path to Authorship

A published book is one of the most influential endorsements of your expertise and thought leadership, and becoming a Trainer naturally leads you to become an author.

The information you share with clients, colleagues, customers, and employees during trainings or in your courses can easily be converted into a book that resonates with thousands of people. Through the delivery of your training sessions, you have had a lot of opportunities to refine your ideas, test your content in front of an audience, gauge their reactions, and course-correct where necessary.

Consequently, you have a high chance of ending up with a successful book that will also serve as a marketing tool for your training programs. Readers of your book will reach out to learn further from you by signing up for your training programs or buying your courses because they have already been impacted by you.

Reason #11
Plan B

Even the most traditional jobs can be unstable. Many people have lost their jobs and not been able to make headway since then. With the economic problems created by COVID-19, there is no gainsaying the fact that everyone needs some stability and a fallback plan. Your income as a Trainer would serve as a good backup option should you lose your job.

Also, your regular job becomes routine after a while, and routine soon gets boring. Challenge yourself by learning more skills that you can teach others. Having a training business on the side can inject excitement into your work life and provide you with a ready option should you decide to quit your full-time job.

Reason #12
Maximised Impact

"I am indebted to my father for living, but to my teacher for living well."
Alexander the Great

You owe it to the world to turn your know-how, your experience, and your expertise into a product or service that people can consume and benefit from. Consider this, virtually every business utilises a Trainer at some point to help build and develop the professional capabilities of their teams. The need for Trainers will only increase as companies begin to rebuild after the devastating effects of COVID-19. Without investing in their employees' talent and professional development, companies risk falling out of pace with their competitors and losing thousands – if not millions – of dollars in unrealised revenue due to a lack of training.

There are some pretty impressive statistics that can help you understand just how important Trainers are to the business world!

• In a Grovo study conducted in 2017, 70% of employees are influenced to stay or leave based on the training and development opportunities offered by their employers.

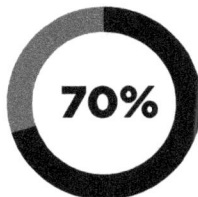

70%

- A study carried out by Gallup showed that insufficient training results in a 13.5 million-dollar loss per 1000 employees.

- Only 1 in 10 employees in the U.S. feel they have the skills required to use the technology needed to do their day-to-day tasks, according to research by Middlesex University for Work-Based Learning.

- The 2018 training industry report shows that average training expenditures for large companies increased from $17 million in 2017 to $19.7 million in 2018. And this is expected to continue rising.

In this chapter, I have laid out many compelling benefits you stand to gain from building a career or business as a Trainer. In the second part of this book, I will lay out clear guidelines on how you can become a damn good Trainer. I will share with you the most potent growth-hacking techniques that I have mastered in the last sixteen years. Have fun with these hacks, as they are incredibly powerful and will give you an advantage over anyone who wants to compete against you.

Key Takeaways

- There are several compelling reasons why you should become a Trainer. One, you can leverage the experience, expertise, and networks you have built over time in your career or business to start making money immediately. Also, if you leverage technology, your training program could be up and running in less than a week.

- Two, you can diversify your income stream. Two-thirds of self-made millionaires have at least three income streams. Today's economy makes this a necessity, not a luxury.

- Three, you can become more effective in your area of expertise. The more you teach a skill, the more proficient you become at it.

- Four increased exposure and visibility as a Trainer can open up new and more significant opportunities for your career advancement or business growth.

- Five, by creating online courses that are available for purchase round the clock, you can generate income while you sleep.

- Six, with low start-up costs and the ability to leverage your current expertise, becoming a Trainer is a clear and viable path to owning your business.

- Seven, due to training always being in demand, it is one of the best ways to generate consistent income and fortify yourself against unexpected income loss in your job or business.

PART 2

BUILDING YOUR TRAINING CAPABILITIES

Build up to breakthrough; to excel as a trainer
you must first go to school

5

YOU MUST FIRST
BECOME A STUDENT

*"In learning, you will teach, and in teaching,
you will learn*

Phil Collins

Recently, a friend of mine expressed her frustration at being what she called a broke expert. "I feel like a fraud." She complained to me. "How can I claim to be an expert, and not know how to extract economic value from my expertise? Yet, I come across so-called experts whose content is average at best, but they are charging a king's ransom and making a killing."

Even though she was a highly celebrated thought leader in her field, beyond the LinkedIn likes, comments, shares and standing ovations at speaking engagements (most of which were unpaid), she barely made any money from her hard work. She had assumed that all she needed to do to be rewarded financially was to show up as an expert. She had not taken the time to study and learn the business side of training and how to profit from her expertise.

Probably the most profound advice I have ever received was from a mentor who told me this: "Whether you're facing your biggest opportunity or your most daunting challenge, always begin the journey by first becoming a student." I took this advice to heart, and it has literally been a game-changer for me in business and in life. Now, I am passing the same advice on to you. If you want to be an exceptionally successful Trainer, thought leader, coach, or consultant, go to "school". Start by learning the ins and outs of your chosen industry and, importantly, discover how to make it profitable.

> *"Whether you're facing your biggest opportunity or your most daunting challenge, always begin the journey by first becoming a student."*

Experts have absolutely no business being broke. None whatsoever. But most are barely making any money from their expertise because they lack the know-how to commercialise and convert it into economic value and financial wealth.

Most of the ingredients required for success are already possessed by these experts. Usually, what they need to tip the scale of success is one missing piece of the puzzle. The Dunning-Kruger Effect describes a situation where someone is blissful in their ignorance. They are ignorant of what they do not know. In other words, they are unaware of the obstacles in their way. If you don't know what you don't know, how will you change it? That is the situation many experts find themselves in. You are best positioned to discover that missing piece when you become a student of your trade.

> *If you don't know what you don't know, how will you change it?*

"When you don't learn the best, you will teach the worst."
Israelmore Ayivor

I am a firm believer that you cannot give what you do not have. If you want to sell, the least that will be expected of you is to learn the business of selling. Training is no different. To become a successful

Trainer, you have to acquire the skills of a Trainer. Sadly, there are a lot of people out there who peddle training or coaching but have no depth whatsoever. Many are hustlers who show up and regurgitate what they have memorised in books but never practised or lived, thinking the ability to talk is all they need to impart knowledge and improve performance. Nothing, of course, can be farther from the truth.

Then, there are those who do bring to the table a wealth of expertise and experience but erroneously believe that is all they need to become successful as Trainers. Knowing something and being able to communicate it so that others can understand and run with it are two completely different things.

When an expert shows up to train people without having the right skills, the needs of the learner end up taking a back seat as the Trainer focuses primarily on his expertise. He will go on and on about his expertise and how simple what he is teaching is, never really pausing to consider that he cannot use his level of expertise as a measuring stick for everyone in the room. They suffer from the curse of knowledge, a cognitive bias that occurs when an individual, teaching others, unknowingly assumes that the students have the background and level of understanding as he does. Naturally, the learner who is struggling to understand the training content soon loses interest or gets bored of hearing about how great the Trainer is (and by implication, how far behind he is), and zones out.

And even if you have developed yourself to become an excellent Trainer, obtaining professional certifications can improve your capabilities tremendously. This was my experience. When I started my training career, I had been running training sessions for about three years without any formal training certification. Then one day, I attended a conference and one of the speakers shared how after about twenty years of training without any professional qualification, she decided to get certified. She said this one decision alone made a tremendous difference in her career and improved her effectiveness by at least 200%.

"The beautiful thing about learning is that nobody can take it away from you."
B.B. King

Fuelled by my strong desire to improve, I enrolled in a training certification course and it was one of the best learning investments I had ever made. Halfway through the first day, I concluded that I owed an apology to everyone I had trained prior to that event. It was, indeed, a perception-expanding experience, and it made me see that my responsibilities as a Trainer start long before a training session begins and continues long afterwards. The program helped me make the much-needed transition from a non-professional who happens to train to a Professional Trainer who has the right skills and tools to help people improve their performance and business results. Whatever is worth doing is what doing exceptionally well, and you can significantly increase your chance of success as a Trainer by investing time, effort and resources into your own training.

So, in order to attain that coveted status of an excellent Trainer that cannot be ignored, what exactly should you go to school to learn and master? Based on my experience of almost twenty years as a Trainer, as well as extensive interactions with hundreds of remarkable Trainers, I highlight below, the non-negotiable curriculum a world-class Trainer must master.

1. Principles, Practices, and Processes of Learning

"Teaching is the highest form of understanding."
Aristotle

As a trainer who intends to bring transformation to people, you must deliver a great learning experience. And to do that, you must be knowledgeable about the learning characteristics, capabilities, and constraints of the people you train. Over the years, extensive research has been carried out to study and improve how adults learn. The results of these studies, including the discovery of learning styles and preferences, are contained in volumes of books that are readily available.

Learning requires change, and it is difficult for adults to change. In fact, the ability of the brain cells to create and store new memories weaken over time. Unlike children who have billions of virgin brain cells waiting to receive and absorb information like sponges, conditioned behaviours, environmental stimuli, ingrained thoughts and emotions in adults reduce the ability of the brain to learn, to create new memories and to develop as they grow older. Therefore, for impactful learning to occur in adults, you, the Trainer, must know how to link new knowledge to existing experiences.

> *Learning requires change, and it is difficult for adults to change.*

Furthermore, you need to understand that every brain is different. Each person has their own unique experiences that have shaped their mind and continue to do so throughout their life. The more you can connect the new behaviour you are teaching to past experiences, the easier it would be for the brain to develop new pathways that lead to the desired change.

Adult learners need practical learning experiences that are designed to produce results in real-life scenarios. You must learn to deliver training that is practical, pragmatic, and easy to apply. Adults want to learn what will help them perform better at work, solve everyday problems, and excel at new skills. They are not looking to acquire knowledge that might never be useful to them.

For adult learning to be effective, training must be "just-in-time" and not "just-in-case." The easier your participants can apply what they have learnt during your training on the job, the more value they will draw from it. One of the hallmarks of an adult learner is the ability to discern between useful and useless information. Adults need to know exactly how their learning can be applied in real-life situations. They need to know why they are being taught a particular knowledge, skill, or competency. You need to communicate this clearly from the beginning.

For adult learning to be effective, training must be "just-in-time" and not "just-in-case."

When adults are learning, their scepticism antenna is perpetually switched on and tuned in to Radio WIIFM (What's In It For Me). Making sure the content is relevant to the needs of your participants is non-negotiable if they are expected to learn as effectively as possible. How will the training help them in their day-to-day activities? How can they apply this knowledge every day? How can they apply it to improve their lives? How can they profit from it? These are very important questions to address comprehensively as a Trainer.

Children are usually self-motivated or can be easily motivated by external factors such as treats and rewards. But it is not easy to motivate an adult who, for most of the day, is preoccupied with conflicting thoughts, worries, and whatnot. Lasting change has to come from within the self, and this is challenging for adults. This obstacle is especially prevalent in company-sponsored training programs, where if the participant feels the training is unnecessary, it becomes more difficult for them to pay adequate attention to their learning. Having a good grasp of how to overcome these hindrances to learning is crucial when designing, developing, and delivering your training programs.

Several great books have been written on the subject of adult learning, and two of my favourites are *Facilitating Learning with the Adult Brain in Mind: A conceptual and Practical Guide* by Kathleen Taylor & Catherine Marienau, and *Adult Learning: Linking Theory and Practice* by Sharan B. Merriam and Laura L. Bierema. I also recommend training programs by institutions such as *Talent Development Association*. These and many other resources are essential study materials for Trainers aspiring to be the best at what they do.

2. Principles, Practices, and Processes of Training

Over the years, training has evolved to become a unique source of strategic advantage for organisations that are discerning enough to embrace it. Breakthrough training programs have delivered undeniable results and helped to propel organisations and individuals to unprecedented levels of performance. But not all programs deliver at this level of effectiveness. Mainly because there are plenty of myths, outdated principles, and inaccurate expectations when it comes to designing and delivering an effective training program.

For your training to be effective, you need to expertly articulate the expected outcomes of the program, track your trainees' progress, and continuously make necessary improvements. Irrespective of how you deliver the training (online or in-person), all the training materials, tools, and resources must work together towards meeting the expected outcomes.

As a trainer, one of your most important responsibilities is to deliver training that drives your client's profit margin or improves their wellbeing. Thus, at the end of every training initiative, you should aim to answer these questions with a "Yes":

i.   the training make a positive difference?

ii. Did it achieve the results for which it was designed?

iii. Was it worth the investment made by your client?

These answers must then be documented and presented back to the sponsor of the training program as evidence, to measure their return of investment (ROI) and return of expectation (ROE).

Although there are several training models available, the same fundamental principles underlie their design, development, and delivery. Just like the subject of adult learning, a lot of studies and research have also been carried out on the principles of effective training. This research has been distilled into numerous books and other training resources. Some favourites of mine include *Telling Ain't Training* by Harold D Stolovitch and Erica J. Keeps, and *The Six Disciplines of Breakthrough Learning* by Wick, Pollock, and Jefferson.

3. The Business and Profession of Training

The training industry is a $400 billion market that is bound to keep expanding in the foreseeable future. Just like any wide-open market, the laws of demand and supply apply here and are responsible for the explosive growth of this industry. As long as organisations and individuals have training needs (and they always will), demand will always outstrip supply. And thankfully, due to its fragmented nature, no single entity can have a monopoly in the Training industry.

There are different population groups that consume training. These consumers make up the pool of your target customers, and you must study them carefully to know who you will serve and how best to serve them. They can be roughly divided into three categories:

i.   Employees of business organisations and government institutions across the federal, state and local levels, ministries and agencies.

ii. Service providers who require continuous training for work registration and practice licenses.

iii. Professionals and business owners who invest in personal development out of pocket, either for the purpose of starting or growing their business, making career transitions or just learning a new vocation.

As a Trainer, you must carry out thorough research into your industry to understand its scope and complexity so that you can position yourself for success and get your piece of the cake. Some books I recommend for learning the business side of training are *Running Training Like a Business* by Van Adelsberg and Trolley, and *How to Market Training and Information* by Don Schrello.

4. Train the Trainer

"Who dares to teach must never cease to learn."
John Cotton Dana

Another hallmark of a professional trainer is the ability to understand that training is not always the solution to a client's performance or developmental problems. There might be an issue with the organisation's policies and processes. Or, the consequence and reward system might need refining. These are problems training cannot solve. Sometimes, wrong hiring is the underlying cause of poor business performance. I recommend reading and implementing the strategies outlined in my book, *Hiring Right – A Matter of Life and Death for Businesses, Business Owners and Executives* to help with this.

No matter how good a Trainer is or how great participants adjudge the learning experience, if the systems and resources needed to perform the newly learnt skills and competencies are not available, performance will not improve. It takes humility and personal integrity for the Trainer to admit this, especially where there is money to be made.

Consequently, when analysing the needs of a client, you have to go through the exercise of proving or disproving training as the best solution for their performance gap. All performance improvement strategies must be duly considered before training is settled upon as the right solution. *Train the Trainer* programs will ensure you are adequately equipped to diagnose what the client really needs and what will help you create training programs that will be of great benefit to them. The exact specification and content of the training certification you choose to pursue will be different, depending on your niche or industry. A highly recommended book along these lines is *Master Trainer Handbook* by Bob Pike.

5. Benchmarking Existing Trainers and Training Models

It was Isaac Newton who said, "If I have seen further than others, it is by standing upon the shoulders of giants." I wish I could tell you that all the ideas I have implemented over the years to grow my training business were my inventions, or that I am some kind of training or business genius. The truth is, I am a collector of great insights and brilliant ideas.

A mentor of mine once told me that he had never had an original idea in his life. "It's just too damn risky." He'd said. Yet he continues to be a hugely successful businessman. The secret of his success was, rather than trying to reinvent the wheel he modelled his business after ideas that had been proven over time. There is really nothing new under the sun. Reinventing the wheel requires you to be a genius, and even then, it carries with it a very high probability of failure. I am no genius, and I hate failing, so I prefer to carefully copy the ideas that have made others successful—at least until I have gotten a very good handle on the basics. This tilts the odds significantly in my favour and gives me a high probability of success.

The statement, "Good artists copy; great artists steal" quoted by Steve Jobs and attributed to Pablo Picasso, is unquestionably a philosophy that has compelled me to collect great insights and brilliant ideas over the years. Yes, there is a place for creativity and invention, but in my opinion, this should come after you have at least mastered the basics.

You stand to significantly increase your chances of success by taking the time to study successful trainers and business models that are already out there. Learn all you can from them and use this to shape how you build your own training programs.

6. Mastery of Your Subject Matter

It goes without saying that you must attain the status of a Subject Matter Expert in your chosen area of training. This is absolutely non-negotiable. Anything short of this and you will find yourself continuously hustling in trying to make headway as a Trainer.

As a subject matter expert, you are the person who has the wealth of knowledge, skills and experience that everyone else needs to glean from. When you demonstrate a keen understanding of your subject area, you naturally inspire and gain the trust of your clients and potential clients. If this foundation is not in place from the start, you face losing your professional credibility along with possible earnings.

And this should not be a one-time achievement. Learning and honing your craft is a continuous, never-ending process for Trainers. You can never stop expanding your capacity as an expert. This is the most basic requirement for all professionals and even more so, Trainers.

> *Learning and honing your craft is a continuous, never-ending process for Trainers*

Key Takeaways

- Being a highly celebrated thought leader without learning how to profit from your expertise can leave you broke and frustrated.

- To commercialise your expertise and extract its true economic value, you must become a student of the training profession and master it as a trade. You cannot rely solely on your expertise to make money or impact people.

- To excel as a Trainer, you must first of all be well versed in the principles that undergird adult learning. The more knowledgeable you are about how your audience best receives and acts on the information shared, the more effective your training programs will be.

- Two, you must be highly skilled at designing, developing, and delivering training programs that generate results for your clients and drive their profit margin.

- Three, you must continually study and learn the business side of training, including marketing, sales, and financial management, to name a few.

- Four, you must never stop mastering your subject matter and expanding your expertise through dedicated self-study and professional certifications.

6

YOU MUST SELECT THE RIGHT NICHE

"I fear not the man who has practised 10,000 kicks once, but I fear the man who has practised one kick 10,000 times."
Bruce Lee

One of the most strategic actions you can take as you begin your journey towards a successful and rewarding career as a Trainer is to determine the market you are best equipped to serve. Almost every business or market leader achieved their success by niching down to one specific area.

What is a niche?

A niche is a predetermined area of specialism that makes economic sense, and you are passionate about and are well equipped for. In other words, it is operating within your "zone of genius." Who are you called to serve, and what problems will you help them solve? A disproportionate

You attract no one when you try to attract everyone!

number of businesses crash before they even make it out of the gate because they are driven by a generalist "Jack-of-all-trades" approach, which assumes that the more areas you serve, the more people you will reach and the more success you will have. Yet, nothing could be farther from the truth. You attract no one when you try to attract everyone!

Choosing Your Training Niche

Experience has taught me that to achieve spectacular success in business, career, or as a thought-leader, specialising in a niche is probably the best approach to adapt. And the more laser-focused your niche, the higher your chances of success. Looking back, I wished I had learned and adopted this principle much earlier. It would surely have made things much less complicated and created more success for my business.

> *"No niche is too small if it is truly yours."*
> Seth Godin

Specialisation is one of the universal laws of life. An individual that does not specialise in their profession risks a mediocre or failed career. A small business that does not specialise will struggle to achieve true greatness. It is better to know and do one thing exceptionally well and at depth than to know many things at surface level. The reasoning behind niching is simple; to be exceptionally successful as a Trainer, you have to be an expert, the best at what you do. And to attain and maintain the status of expertise, you need to invest disproportionate amounts of time, energy, and money into developing yourself. Since these resources are not unlimited, you gain advancements faster when you zero in on one or two areas of speciality, rather than spreading yourself too thin.

Not picking a niche or choosing one that does not align with your context or reality is a huge mistake and it amounts to what is commonly referred to as "undisciplined pursuit of more". This is the number one reason most businesses fail, and many careers stagnate. You must pick a niche and go on to become so good at it; you simply cannot be ignored.

There is a common belief that the wider your target area, the more clients you have the potential to secure. This is a very tempting but misleading idea. For example, a Trainer desperately tries to secure contracts from every organisation within the state he lives in, regardless of size, industry or training needs. Unfortunately, by casting her net too wide and hoping for a catch, she ends up wasting valuable time and resources. In her attempt to connect with the broadest possible audience, her message resonates with no one in particular. And even worse, because she lacks the clarity needed to identify and connect with her ideal clients, she ends up alienating them.

If generalist marketing is like casting a net and hoping for whatever might come along, then niching is like using the right bait to attract a specific kind of fish. This kind of marketing stands out from the crowd and resonates with exactly the type of people you are trying to attract.

A training program that caters to a carefully chosen niche would focus on a specific group of people and therefore, be tailored to perfectly suit their needs. Furthermore, when starting out and there are other more established training providers in your industry, you can eliminate some of the competition by focusing your limited resources on a narrow and specific training need.

There are two brilliant approaches you can adopt when deciding on the niche you want to pick and the type of Trainer you would like to become. Usually, people adopt one or the other, but I recommend combining both for maximum clarity and effectiveness. These approaches are:

1. Inside-out Approach

2. Outside-in Approach

> *"We are all experts in our own little niches."*
> Alex Trebek

Inside-Out Approach

The inside-out approach is a business growth strategy that directs an organisation to look inward and clearly identify its core competencies, which should then be mastered and leveraged to beat the competition. In identifying your ideal niche, you can apply this strategy by clearly defining your inner strengths and capabilities – where your passion lies, and how you can leverage them to become a successful Trainer. There are three key questions you must answer as part of the Inside-Out approach.

i. What are you passionate about? What areas of focus excite you?

ii. What do you have the potential to achieve mastery in or to become the very best at?

iii. What makes economic sense, has the potential to meet your financial needs and will enable you live the type of life you want to live?

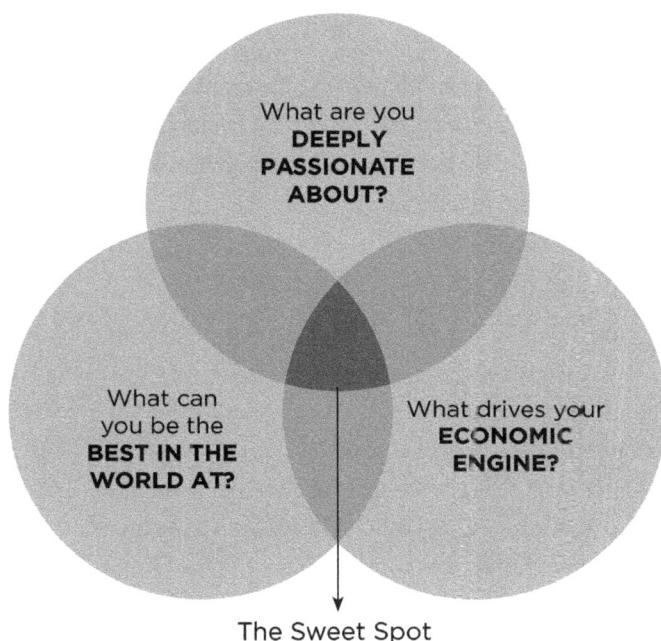

The Sweet Spot

FIGURE 3: The Inside Out Approach

Where the three sections intersect, as shown above, is your sweet spot and should become your area of focus. In doing this exercise, it is also crucial that the three circles are given equal consideration. Leaving even one out can lead to catastrophic failure. Here are three possible scenarios if all three questions are not carefully considered.

- If you choose a niche you are not passionate about, you are unlikely to enjoy it enough to invest the rigour and sacrifice required to achieve mastery and become the best at it.

- If you do not pick the niche that you are able to achieve mastery in and become the best at, you are unlikely to be passionate about it or make a lot of money from it.

- If your work does not consistently meet your financial aspirations, it is unlikely you will possess the drive and financial capacity to achieve mastery over the long haul.

To help you further in identifying the right niche using the Inside-Out approach, the Success and Happiness Peaks exercise is a great tool I also recommend. (Visit the website **www.youmustbecomeatrainer.com** to download the template).

Success Peaks

This is based on the idea that you are more likely to succeed where you have been successful in the past. Therefore, a good place to start is by cataloguing your previous successes. Take time to reflect on your professional or business journey so far and identify your success peaks. These are the areas where you have been very successful, where you have achieved meaningful results and have been highly celebrated. List as many of these areas as you can.

Happiness Peaks

Once you have identified the areas where you are likely to replicate the successes from your past, it is time to find out what makes you happy. The happiness peak is based on the belief that you are more likely to be passionate about what makes you happy. So, take time to reflect and identify your happiness peaks. These are the seasons of your life when you were happiest. What activities or work were you engaged in during these periods? List as many as you can.

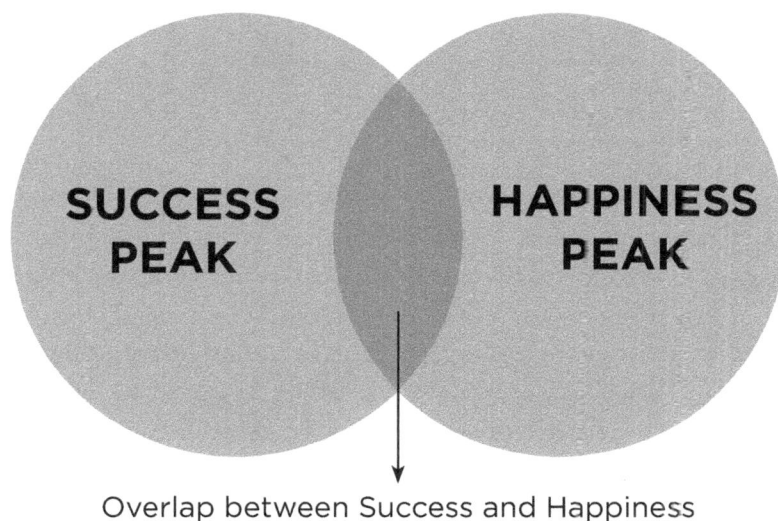

Overlap between Success and Happiness

FIGURE 4: Success and Happiness Peaks

Now, look at the two lists from the Inside-Out and the Success & Happiness Peaks exercises. Are there any overlaps? Can you see any common threads running through the lists? The intersection between the two lists is where you will find the niche that you can be passionate about and can also achieve tremendous success in. This will be the area that, if focused on will get you buzzing with excitement and will significantly increase your chances of success.

Outside-in Approach

One piece of advice we hear a lot nowadays is, "Follow your passion." But it is never really that simple. Just because we hear of successful people who got to where they are by following their passion does not automatically mean success lies at the end of every pursuit of one's passions. In fact, the ones who make it to the top "following their passion" are a tiny minority compared to those who failed. Statistics show that about eighty percent of businesses fail in their first year. And another fifty percent fail before their fifth year. These are men and women who started out with the best of intentions, who followed their passions but who never made it to the other side.

Without a doubt, passion is important. It is essential to identify the interests that will drive your success. But you should also pay close attention to the market. While you may have found your passion – the work you would do even if you did not get paid for it – your financial economy must not be side-lined. You need to get paid for what you do and so, adopting an inside-out approach only can be risky. To balance it out, you need to go one step further from what you want, to what the market wants. Since you will not be training or paying yourself, it is crucial to uncover what the market needs and is willing to pay for.

> *You need to get paid for what you do and so, adopting an inside-out approach only can be risky.*

The Outside-In approach drives growth by looking outward. You actively research markets, customer choices, and the competition. Then, you create business offerings designed to beat the competition and cater to the needs of your clients. Deploying this strategy will help you identify what the market is willing to pay for.

While many trainers are product-driven and some are sales-driven, very few are market-driven. The highest value you can create and capture in business is directly proportional to how intelligently you can read and interpret market trends. You should be asking: what opportunities are out there? What does the competition look like? Do I have what it takes to beat the competition? This is so important.

The Four Ps of Marketing is a framework developed by marketing professionals to determine how successful an idea will be in the marketplace. These Ps are Product, Pricing, Place, and Promotion. Unfortunately, they left out the most crucial P for creating market success – The Problem.

If you have an in-depth understanding of the problem the market you intend to serve is facing, you can positively influence the remaining Ps of marketing. If you design an excellent program that does not address real market problems, no one will buy it. This is commonly referred to as Solutionist Thinking – a situation where one first creates a solution and then goes searching for a problem. The market is only willing to pay you to solve real and urgent problems, so in picking your niche, you must identify and select the problem you will solve.

> *If you design an excellent program that does not address real market problems, no one will buy it.*

Usually, there are several problems in any given market. Therefore, you need to ask this critical question: Which problems am I most suited to solve? And the answer to this question is out there. It is not in your head. It is not in your office space. It is not on your computer system. It is out there in the market. You must go out there and engage with the market. You will not learn anything staying in your house or sitting at your desk. The solution to how you will succeed as a Trainer is out there. You need to engage and interact regularly with the market. You need to devise a systematic process for listening to and understanding the market. A process that is deliberate, proactive, well-structured, and consistent. Anything short of this approach will simply not do.

Take, for example, in writing this book. One of the first things I did was to carry out extensive research into common challenges faced by Trainers. The findings from that research are the main reason you are reading this book.

If you do not take anything from this section, please remember this – a Trainer is nothing but a problem solver. And the nature of the problem you solve and how you solve it is determined by the market, not you.

How to Find Market Problems

You can discover market problems by engaging with existing and potential clients, or even people who may never buy your services. By observing people who are not your ideal customers, you might learn how not to present your offers! The wider you cast your fishing net when researching, the more you discover about your target market.

Below are some of the questions you should ask people when researching into market problems:

i. What is the biggest problem you or your organisation is trying to solve at the moment?

ii. Why is it so crucial for you to solve this problem?

iii. How painful is this problem?

iv. What are the consequences of not solving the problem?

v. What success are you likely to achieve if you are able to solve the problem?

vi. How are you currently coping with the problem?

vii. When you solve the problem' what will success look like? What will be your ideal situation?

To succeed spectacularly, you need to become a market expert. You need to spend quality time with customers to identify their real problems instead of theorising about what their problems could or should be. You can also find out more about the market problem from people that frequently interact with the market, such as salespeople, customer service executives, and so on. Through this, you can measure satisfaction, find unresolved problems, and discover hidden preferences. You must commit to consistently, continuously, and unrelentingly using the outside-in approach to bring market perspectives to bear on whatever you do. This is absolutely non-negotiable.

Your career or business should exist to solve market problems. Market-driven careers or businesses define what they do in terms of the specific problems they solve for specific customers or markets. I have seen Trainers fall in love with their products and services and describe what they do in terms of their specialisation or area of expertise. As a result, they alienate potential clients. Don't make that mistake. Don't fall in love with your products or services. Your product or service offerings does not have the money to pay you. Your customers do. Falling in love with your product and service offering is a recipe for failure. Instead, fall madly in love with the problems you will solve for your target market.

> *Falling in love with your product and service offering is a recipe for failure.*

Characteristics of the problems you should solve

Not every problem is worth solving. No matter how passionate you are about what you are offering, if there are not enough people who care enough to invest their time and money into getting it solved, your idea will fail. The existence of a market is not enough. There must be a significant market share for your proposed idea to succeed. In finding the right problems to solve, you should be able to answer the following questions in the affirmative:

1. Is the problem pervasive?

If there are only a handful of people experiencing the problem, then the growth of your business will automatically be capped. Any sustainable business model would require you to charge significantly high fees to make up for the small market. Then, there is the competition to consider. If it is indeed a problem worth solving and people are willing to pay for it, then certainly you can expect competition. You could end up in a highly saturated market where the ratio of businesses to customers is unsustainably high. But, if the problem is widespread – or has the potential to grow, your business is more likely to survive the test of time.

2. Is the problem urgent in nature?

Is the problem one that people cannot live with and are determined to solve quickly? Most people tend to put problems off until they become urgent or critical. One of the tactics life insurance salesmen use is to target people who have faced some form of life-threatening event such as a car accident, or a health scare. They know death seems a long way off for most people and trying to sell insurance to a thirty-year-old man who believes he will live till eighty is an uphill task. So, they look for opportunities that bring the prospect of death closer to home. Does the market consider the problem urgent? Or will people keep putting it off and never really commit their resources to getting it solved? If it is the latter, you will need to come up with creative ways to convince the market to act now.

3. Are the clients willing to pay to solve it?

Now, no matter how widespread the problem is or how urgently people want it solved, if you target an audience that is unwilling – or unable – to pay for your solution, then you do not have a business. For example, trying to sell a 2,000 US Dollars home interior design course to an audience of bargain-hunting DIY enthusiasts might not be the greatest idea.

Researching Your Ideal Customers

When I founded my training company, the first thing my team and I did was to look at our strengths. We reflected on our journey to identify our core areas of strength, where we had crossed the line of unquestionable competence.

The next question we asked was, "Which industry or company

would benefit from our wealth of knowledge, experience and expertise?" We researched the market to find problems that were worth solving and matched our core competencies.

Then we drilled down even further. We went beyond identifying the right organisations to the departments within them that would specifically need our training interventions. Who would be eager to listen if we put together a value proposition to solve those problems and take them from point A (where they were currently) to point B (where they wanted to be)? We invested a lot of time and resources into securing the right answers to that question. This was how we were able to identify our ideal clients.

And finally, we needed to get our offers right. We also needed to articulate them in a way that was most likely to attract the attention of our prospects. We learnt to write proposals in a way that would resonate most with them. We interviewed staff at those organisations and asked for their opinions about our programs. We also asked how they would convince their organisations to enrol them on our training programs. We took some of the words they used in describing the benefits they would get from the program and used them verbatim in the proposals we sent out. We did not want to start from scratch by cold calling prospects, so we targeted the contacts we already had within those organisations and went through them to get to the key people. These are some of the tactics that helped us secure clients without coming across as sales sharks.

When approaching prospects as part of your research into your ideal customers, here is a guideline that will help you maximise each opportunity.

i. **Assure them**

- Let them know you are not selling.

- For credibility, showcase unquestionable competence and expertise.

      – Ask questions about the problems they are facing.

ii. **Ask them**

      – What drives you crazy?

      – What informs your buying decision?

      – What great solutions have you seen lately?

      – Who is my competition, and what do you think of them?

      – What do you think of my products and services?

iii. **Understand them**

      – What are their KPIs – Key Performance Indicators?

      – How is their performance measured? What makes them earn a promotion or bonus?

      – What helps them shine in their space?

      – What will support their growth and advancement?

      – What will increase their sense of fulfilment?

iv. **Observe them**

      – Watch them interact with your (or similar) products or services.

      – Observe and document a day in the life of your customer. Understand that even if they do not yet know it is a problem, as long as it is impacting them negatively, it can be profitable for you when developing a solution that will solve that problem.

Putting it all together

Once you have collated the results – the list of potential niches – from the Inside-Out and Outside-In exercises, you can then select your ideal niche from the overlap between the two. In other words, what niche are you passionate about that also has high market value and demand? If you can find that niche, then you have certainly hit the jackpot. That is your sweet spot and you should focus on it disproportionately.

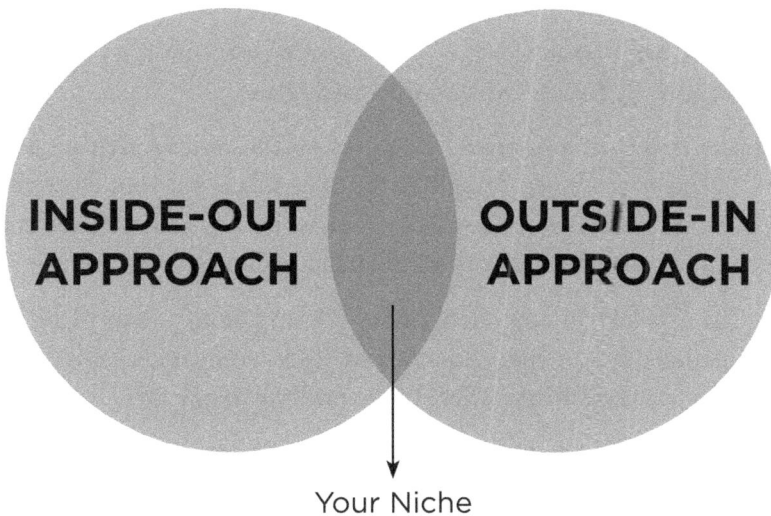

INSIDE-OUT APPROACH

OUTSIDE-IN APPROACH

Your Niche

FIGURE 5: Your Niche

Key Takeaways

- A niche or your 'zone of genius' is the area of specialism that you are passionate about, well equipped to serve, and that has a high market value.

- Identifying the niche you are best equipped to serve is the foundational step towards building a successful and rewarding career or business as a Trainer. The more specialised and laser-focused your niche is, the greater your chances of success.

- There are two approaches you can deploy in finding your best niche – the Inside-Out and the Outside-In.

- The Inside-Out approach requires you to clearly identify and leverage your inner strengths to become successful. Pinpoint what you are passionate and excited about, where you can gain mastery, and what can best drive your financial aspirations.

- The Outside-In approach guides you to identify your niche by intelligently studying and interpreting market trends. What does the market need and what are they willing to pay for?

- By combining the Inside-Out and Outside-In approaches, you will significantly increase your chances of picking a training niche that you are passionate about and can make money from.

7

YOU MUST DESIGN YOUR TRAINING PROGRAM FOR SUCCESS

"Learning experiences are like journeys. The journey starts where the learning is now and ends when the learner is successful. The end of the journey isn't knowing more; it's doing more."

Julie Dirksen

During the Second World War, the US Army deployed fighter jets to fire missiles and take out key targets within enemy territories as part of their battle strategy. This seemed like a brilliant idea, but most of the Air Force pilots were missing their targets by an unbelievably wide margin. Needless to say, this was a major concern for the top military brass. The missed targets were not only costing them billions of dollars in wastage but if not addressed quickly, was likely to cost them the war.

In response to this crisis, they launched an investigation into the failed bombing attempts. They discovered that there was a small number of pilots who had a consistently high rate of success in hitting their targets, even though they had the same equipment and were operating under the same conditions as the others. This led them to ask a simple question, "What if we could understand what the successful pilots are doing well and then teach it to all the other pilots?"

In their relentless pursuit of an answer to this question, they reached out to the university community for help in creating a standardised, repeatable, and scalable training program that would help every pilot operate at the same level of efficiency as the handful who were getting it right. Out of the various options presented, the US Army appointed Florida State University's Systematic Design of Instruction program as the winning bid. Almost as soon as it was approved and deployed, they started seeing improvements. Suddenly, fighter pilots who were missing targets before the intervention were becoming more precise at an accelerated pace. Mistakes were drastically reduced. The program was a huge success, and it was not long before the US Army deployed it for all their military training activities.

On seeing the success of the program with the US Army, the healthcare community adopted it to standardise surgeries by designing a step by step guide for surgical operations. It completely revolutionised the surgical community and led to a reduction in surgical errors and loss of life.

This standardised approach to training has evolved over time into what is now called Instructional Design Principles and has become the cornerstone of the learning process in many renowned industries and institutions. It quite simply provides an avenue for expertise to be transferred from one group of people to another without losing its effectiveness in the process. It is a proven way of delivering quality, for maintaining consistency of performance, and increasing the overall efficiency of a system.

"Training programs shouldn't be designed to deliver competence; they must be dedicated to producing excellence. Serious organizations don't aspire to be comfyortabl above average."
Brandon Webb

What is Instructional Design?

Instructional design is the creation of suitable training exercises for the acquisition and application of knowledge and skills. It covers the entire training process from analysis of learning needs to the creation of an efficient system to meet those needs. By designing the training experience, you are able to create guideposts that lead learners through your content in a structured way and helps them acquire the information and skills they need to succeed.

Over the years, several Instructional Design methodologies have been introduced to the world. But by far, the most comprehensive and effective of them all, in my own opinion, is the ADDIE process of Instructional Design. I recommend it highly when designing your training program.

The ADDIE Training Model

When the US Army set out to create a training program for their fighter pilots, they came up with a five-step training model named ADDIE, which is an acronym for the five stages of the training process:

- Analysis
- Design
- Development

- Implementation

- Evaluation

To date, many existing Instructional design models including software development and project management are based on ADDIE. When implemented effectively, ADDIE is a brilliant iterative system that provides feedback for continuous improvement until all the learning needs have been addressed. The rest of this chapter describes in detail the various phases of the ADDIE framework and their application to the design of learning initiatives.

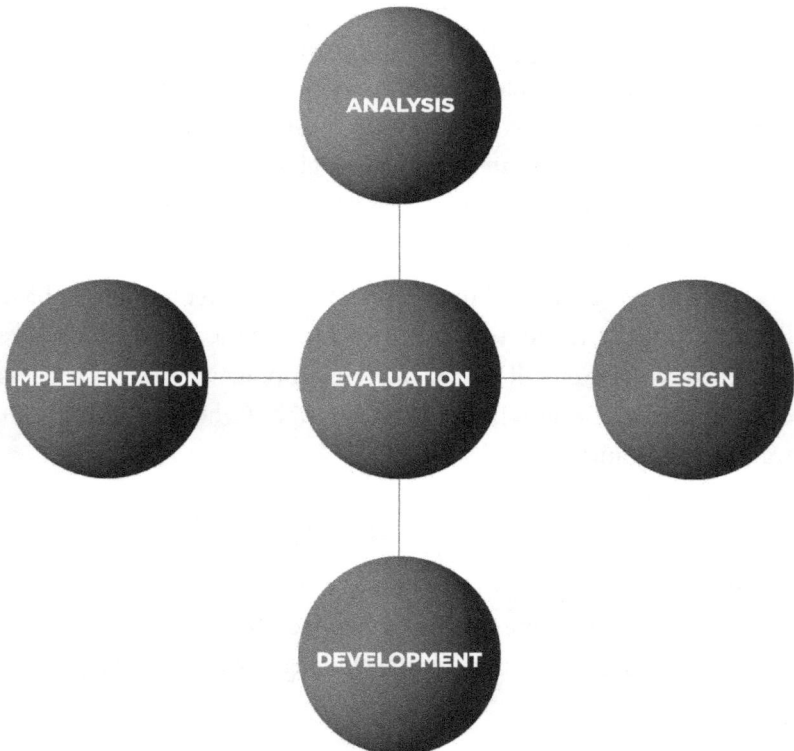

FIGURE 6: The ADDIE Framework

Phase 1: Analysis

The first phase of ADDIE is *Analysis* and can be likened to a medical consultation where a doctor asks the patient pointed questions about their symptoms, the illness, and their medical history. Just as the doctor gathers crucial information in order to diagnose and prescribe the right care for the patient, this phase ensures a trainer has all the information required to accurately define where the organisation is going and how it will get there.

The *Analysis* phase begins with asking and answering critical questions such as, what is the underlying cause of this gap we are trying to fill? What are the goals and expectations of the training program? What media and methodologies will be used? What has worked in the past? What has not? This simple checklist called *5W's and an H* will help you carry out the *Analysis* stage of ADDIE:

- Who is going to get trained? (Analysis of trainees)

- What will the training be centred on? (Context of the training)

- When is it going to happen? (Timeframe)

- Where is it going to happen? (Delivery channels)

- Why are you doing this? (Training objectives)

- How are you going to achieve this? (Methodology & Requirements)

For best practice, these questions should be asked across the three layers – Organisation, Performance, and Performer. At the organisational level, you are looking to gain clear insight into the business, its needs and the training program requested. *What are the business goals? What exactly is the business trying to achieve? What does the business need? Why do they want training?* Typically, the needs of a business fall into four categories: to create something new, something better, something more

> *Typically, the needs of a business fall into four categories: to create something new, something better, something more efficient, or something cheaper.*

efficient, or something cheaper. Which of these is their chief aim? As a Trainer, you absolutely need to be adept at understanding the needs of your clients. This information will help you choose the right training intervention and develop a first-class program that caters effectively to their needs down to the most basic elements such as the stories you will share during the training session. Although technically, you are not training the business directly, by equipping the performer (staff, executives etc.) to gain the right competencies, you are helping the business achieve its goals.

Also, remember that training might not be the only solution to the needs identified by an organisation. In fact, it is usually the case that other non-training interventions such as coaching, recruitment, process automation, and technology upgrades will be required. By committing to this first step of thoroughly analysing the situation at the organisational level, you will be able to develop a holistic view of how best your client's problems can be addressed.

At the Performance level, your goal is to uncover what it would take to break down the organisation's overarching goals and objectives into meaningful actions and tasks that can be carried out by the Performer.

At the Performer level, you find out all you can about the person or people who are designated to attend your training session and subsequently, will be responsible for carrying out the actions that will lead to the agreed objectives. You can discover more about the Performer by asking questions such as, who are the performers? What capabilities do they have? How do they like to learn? What is their current performance status? Is the learner capable of executing set objectives based on their previous performance?

Phase 1 is all about effective diagnosis which is a crucial first step in determining the best way to solve any problem, especially performance related ones.

Phase 2 – Design

The next phase in the ADDIE model is when theory (Analysis) is converted into an actionable plan (Design). During this phase, a detailed plan is designed to show clearly how the training program will address the needs identified during the *Analysis* phase. Likening this to a medical examination, after a doctor establishes the patient's history and carries out a thorough physical examination, he writes a care plan for the relevant medical professionals to put into effect. This care plan might include diagnostic tests, prescriptions, or lifestyle advice. Just like the medical care plan ensures that all the patient's medical needs are met, a design plan should provide a dashboard-like overview of the entire training process and ensure that every training objective is accounted for. Some of the important elements a design plan should address are as follows:

- **Teaching points**

    What is the key information that needs to be passed across?

- **Strategy**

    What methodology and delivery methods will you employ, for example video, online, classroom, one-to-one, etc.?

- **Execution**

    What activities will be carried out as part of the training process? What tools and resources will participants need to access the training and to implement it afterwards? How will you ensure engagement and knowledge retention?

- **Evaluation**

    How will the effectiveness of the program be measured and reviewed? What are the expected outcomes? What will success look like?

- **Timeframe**

  How long is the program expected to run for? How much time will learners need to complete the course?

- **Cost**

  What will it cost? Remember to include indirect costs such as labour, outsourced creatives, travel, studio fees, etc.

Phase 3 – Development

During the development stage, you flesh out your design plan by creating learning objectives that will act as strategic guideposts to help participants do their part in accomplishing agreed objectives. In addition to serving as a guidepost, the learning objectives will be used to measure what participants should be able to do by the end of the training.

Writing clear learning objectives helps you strip off non-essential content and ensures that training content is aligned with the expectations of the program. Unlike the design plan, which begins at the organisational level and works down to the performer, learning objectives start at the participant level and intricately builds up to the overarching vision at organisational level. To design effective learning objectives, there are three core questions you should explore.

i.   What will the learners be able to do by the end of the course? Or, what should participants be able to do when they return to work/ their business?

ii. What are the tools and resources they need to execute the job? Or, what are the conditions necessary for successful implementation?

iii. How will you know when they have done the job and how well they have done it? In other words, there should be success criteria that will act as a guide for meeting objectives at organisational level.

The Four Parts of a Learning Objective

A method that I highly recommend when you are constructing learning objectives for your training program is the ABCD model. It is a simple structure that guides you through the four components that must be in place to ensure the learning objective is clear, actionable, and measurable. Those four components are Audience, Behaviour, Condition, and Degree of Mastery.

Audience

Identify your audience. Who is the intended learner and how will you address them? Typically, trainers use generic words like "learner" or "participant", but if it will add value to the program, it is also possible to go further by describing the learner in more detail by using, for example, his or her job specification.

Behaviour

Identify the key learning points. What performance is the learner expected to exhibit after the training? Ideally, the behaviour should closely reflect real-life tasks the learner will have to perform at the end of the training. Also, it should be measurable and described using action verbs that are well suited to the level of performance expected. If it is an **attitude** that should be adopted, use words like critique, justify, verify, assess, advocate, choose, evaluate, or recommend. For example, "The learner will be able to distinguish between the five stages of..." If **skill** acquisition is the aim, use words such as solve, improve, design, etc. And lastly, if the goal is to remember or reproduce **knowledge** gained or understood, use words like describe, comprehend, identify, copy, or record.

Condition

Identify the rules that will guide the performance. What are the conditions or constraints (if any) under which the learners will be expected to perform the tasks? For example, the learner may be restricted to using data gathered within a specific timeframe to complete their task.

Degree of Mastery

Identify the degree of proficiency required. How well will the learner be required to perform the task? This will largely be the agreed standard of performance and should be clearly stated in measurable forms such as percentage, time, proportion, etc. For example, "… minimum accuracy of 80%."

An ABCD Learning Objective Sample

LEARNING OBJECTIVE	FOUR COMPONENTS
On completion of the ISD session, Trainers will be able to write learning objectives that specify Audience, Behaviour, Condition, and Degree of Mastery (following the ABCD methodology) with a minimum accuracy of 80% in the practice exam.	**Audience:** *Trainers* **Behaviour:** *will be able to write learning objectives that clearly specify Audience, Behaviour, Condition, and Degree of Mastery* **Condition:** *following the ABCD methodology session* **Degree of Mastery:** *with a minimum accuracy level of 80% in the practice exam.*

Phase 4 – Implementation

Once you have completed the analysis, design, and development phases, you have to test the viability of the program before you roll it out on a large scale. Skipping this is risky. If a training program that sounds great on paper does not catch on with the market, you could end up losing vast amounts of time, money and energy invested into building and launching it.

The first step in the implementation stage is to conduct beta tests with a small group of people who are closely matched to your target audience. These beta tests help you gain valuable insight into how the training could perform in real life. You want to know if the program works. If it does not, what are the mitigating factors that can be addressed or eliminated? If it does work, what are the success factors that can be replicated or amplified?

Essentially, you are searching for answers to questions such as, what is the best way to deliver the training based on the learning objectives? What are the most effective instructional techniques, strategies, methods, and media to deploy? What would work best for my learners?

Like the process implemented when introducing a new vaccine, where it is first tested on a small sample of the population before distributing it extensively, you should actively use feedback from the beta tests to revise and improve the program.

Once you have successfully implemented the relevant feedback from the beta tests and are happy enough with the current model of the training, then you are ready to launch it as a full program.

Phase 5 – Evaluation

Although named as a distinct phase, evaluation is actually built into every phase of the ADDIE model from initial analysis through to full implementation. It is important to get feedback at every stage and on every aspect of the training so that you can make continual improvements. There are five levels at which the evaluation of a training program should be carried out. These include:

i.   Reaction: Did participants like and enjoy it?

ii. Learning: Did they learn?

iii. Application: Were they able to apply what they learnt?

iv. Business Impact: Were they able to improve the bottom line?

v. ROI: What was the return on investment for stakeholders?

Evaluation is crucial to the success of your training program. Quite simply, what you cannot measure, you cannot improve. A continuous cycle of evaluation and improvement will ensure that your training program continues to be relevant and valuable to the market.

Key Takeaways

- The ADDIE process of Instructional Design is a comprehensive methodology widely used in designing world-class training programs. Originating from the US Army, ADDIE represents the five stages of the training design process including Analysis, Design, Development, Implementation and Evaluation.

- The Analysis phase is diagnostic. By asking the right questions, you develop a holistic view of your client's needs at the organisational, performance and performer levels.

- At the Design phase, you convert the results of your analysis into a detailed and actionable plan that clearly states how your training program will address the needs identified.

- At the Development phase, your design plan is fleshed out into clear, actionable and measurable learning objectives.

- To craft effective learning objectives, you must be guided by the Audience (intended learners), Behaviour (attitudes, skills or knowledge to be taught), Condition (rules that govern performance) and Degree of Mastery (the proficiency level expected).

- During the Implementation phase, it is important to determine the viability of your training program by first running beta tests. Once the findings and feedback from the tests have been incorporated, the full program is ready to be launched.

- Evaluation should be integrated into all five phases from initial analysis through to full implementation. Creating a system of continuous review and improvement is essential for achieving long term success with your training program.

8

YOU MUST MASTER THE ART OF TRAINING DELIVERY

"The mediocre teacher tells. The good teacher explains. The superior teacher demonstrates. The great teacher inspires."
William Arthur Ward

Perhaps, the greatest improvement in the effectiveness and impact of my training programs came after I began to pay attention to not just *what* I was teaching – the content of my training, but *how* I was delivering it. I have observed and concluded over time that no matter how superb your content is, if you are unable to communicate it to your audience in a way they can easily receive, understand and assimilate it, your impact as a trainer will be severely limited.

It was this realisation that launched me into an extensive search for the best practices in training delivery. And that is what this chapter focuses on. I recommend that you study it carefully and apply what you learn the first opportunity you get. Practising the strategies and tips shared throughout this book, and especially in this chapter, is the best way to set yourself up for success as a Trainer.

The Foundational Rules of Training Delivery

The term "training" is often used to describe the act of teaching an individual or group of persons to acquire knowledge, skills or abilities. To train means to provoke learning by stimulating knowledge and sharing experience, rather than by instruction. A Trainer takes on the role of both a leader and a guide within the classroom. He is not just there to instruct. His job is to help his students achieve the best possible outcomes by encouraging full engagement with the training content, by promoting mutual clarity and understanding, and by skilfully directing their learning towards the training objectives. He inspires them to do their best thinking and to take definite steps in applying the concepts learnt.

To be a good Trainer, there are a few ground rules that should be followed as standard. Perhaps the most important rule is that you must be the best-prepared person in the room. If you are unprepared, it will most likely affect your confidence and your participants will surely pick up on that. If they lose their trust in your ability to deliver the training, it would be difficult to get them to fully engage with you.

In preparation for your training session, there are four critical things you must do. First, you must study your subject matter thoroughly. Second, you must have a detailed plan of how you will deliver the training content. Third, you must organise your materials and all logistics in a way that ensures your content is delivered according to plan. And last, you must be prepared mentally and physically for the demands of the session.

In addition to being well prepared for the training session, you should set the pace and direction of the conversations, use the training time efficiently, and create an atmosphere that is conducive to learning.

Without these foundational rules in place, the training session will fall flat and as most people tend to react in that situation, you will default to delivering a one-sided training where you talk at the participants and throw facts at them without really carrying them along

Understanding How Adults Learn

You may have noticed that the standard rules highlighted above focus primarily on the Trainer and the training environment. They are designed to act as a guide for the Trainer, ensuring both the Trainer and his classroom are up to par. As already mentioned, without these in place, it is almost impossible to put together a successful training program.

To be an excellent Trainer however, your attention must widen beyond yourself and your classroom to include the learners. You must exercise due diligence in finding out as much about the participants as possible. And perhaps, the most crucial information you need to know about the learner is how they actually learn!

In 1968, American educator Malcolm Knowles carried out extensive research into the way adults learn in comparison to children. His research brought into view notable differences between the way the two groups learn. He went on to popularise what is known as the adult learning theory. Prior to that, extensive research had been conducted into studying how children learn, and most people just assumed that the same findings applied to adults. Knowles concluded his research by identifying five principles of adult learning, as well as the learning styles and strengths that are unique to adults.

To walk into a room and deliver a training based on faulty assumptions will not only prove ineffective, but it could be downright disastrous. The best trainings (that deliver the best outcomes for both Trainer and trainee) are the ones where the content and delivery have been expertly matched to the audience. It is crucial that you pay close attention to the five adult learning principles and more importantly, take time to understand how you can utilise them in delivering your training for effective outcomes.

"Where my reason, imagination, or interest were not engaged, I would not or could not learn."
Sir Winston Churchill

The Five Principles of Adult Learning

1. Self-Awareness

Adults are more advanced in their development of self-awareness and emotional maturity compared to children, so it can generally be assumed that they are more independent in their learning. As a result, it rarely goes down well with adults if a training is overly prescriptive and leaves no room for them to have a say in the content or method of learning.

Unlike children who are more open to gaining new knowledge even if the relevance of it is not immediately apparent, adults are more sceptical about receiving new information. This, to a great extent, impacts their willingness to embrace that information or skill and to take it further into application. As a Trainer, your goal is to help participants take ownership of their own learning. This can usually be accomplished by thoroughly researching your audience and understanding what makes them tick. Are they senior leaders or entry-level? Are they millennials or Generation X? What are they expecting to get out of the session? All these factors should play a part in how you deliver the training.

2. Previous Learning Experiences

Over time, adults accumulate a vast reservoir of experiences, compared to children who have a more limited experience of life. When exposed to new information, an adult will draw from their past experiences to decipher or enhance that information. Adults tend to interpret information in light of what they already know. Tapping into an adult learner's wealth of experiences can be a powerful way to enrich your training sessions. You can do this by structuring your content delivery in a way that encourages learners to participate during the training, for example, through discussions and problem-solving activities. You can also use a variety of open questions designed to get learners thinking; the more they think, the more they are likely to dip into their reservoir of knowledge.

When exposed to new information, an adult will draw from their past experiences to decipher or enhance that information.

Endeavour to celebrate the value participants bring to the session. Adult learners need and deserve to be respected for their knowledge and life experiences. Creating a learning environment that encourages them to share their experiences (including mistakes and regrets) helps increase their motivation to learn. Furthermore, you need to understand that every brain is different. Each person has their own unique experiences that have shaped their views and will continue to do so throughout their life. The more you can connect the new behaviour you are teaching to your participants' past experiences, the easier it would be for the brain to develop new pathways that will lead to the desired change.

3. Readiness to Learn

Adults tend to be more receptive and engaged in learning when they can see the relevance of that training to their job or personal life. Otherwise, they may see it as a waste of time and switch off. One question you must therefore ask is, 'In what way is this content important to the learner?" Ensure you continually emphasise the relevance of the training to the participant's goals and objectives.

Always be sure to ask adult learners what they expect to get out of the training at the beginning of the session. Then, tailor the key discussion points to address those expectations throughout the training. The more you demonstrate how the topics can make each participant better and more successful in their personal and the organisational pursuits, the more motivated they will be to learn and participate in the training.

For example, if a group of sales managers want a training on how to expand their customer base and ultimately increase sales, the first thing you want to unearth is their real motivation for wanting more sales. What is the reward for hitting their sales targets? Is it a promotion, or a bonus, or more high-profile clients? If you take the time to truly understand the driving force behind their thirst for knowledge, you can use it as a reference point during the training to keep them engaged and willing to learn.

4. Orientation to Learning

It is safe to assume that the predominant question in the mind of most participants during a training is, how can I apply this to my job (or my life)? Adults need to know exactly how you can help them, as well as how the learning can be applied beyond the classroom. They need to know why they are being taught a particular knowledge, skill, or competency. You need to communicate this clearly from the beginning. Your training must cater to this by ensuring it is practical, pragmatic, and application focused.

It should be task- and problem-oriented rather than focused solely on sharing knowledge.

Adults want to learn what will help them perform better at work, solve everyday problems and excel at new skills, not just to acquire knowledge that might never be useful to them. Your training should be delivered in such a way that it connects with the business and life goals, performance objectives, and challenges of your audience. It should be task- and problem-oriented rather than focused solely on sharing knowledge.

Be deliberate about incorporating specific action steps into your training that will help participants achieve results in the context of their objectives.

5. Motivation to Learn

Probably the most formidable hurdle to scale when training adults is a lack of motivation. Conditioned responses to given scenarios are already hardwired into the brain of an adult, so for new information to be acted upon, motivation must be present. You must carefully plan how you will deliver your training so that your audience is not only motivated to engage with the training content, but to retain and apply it after the training.

Probably the most formidable hurdle to scale when training adults is a lack of motivation.

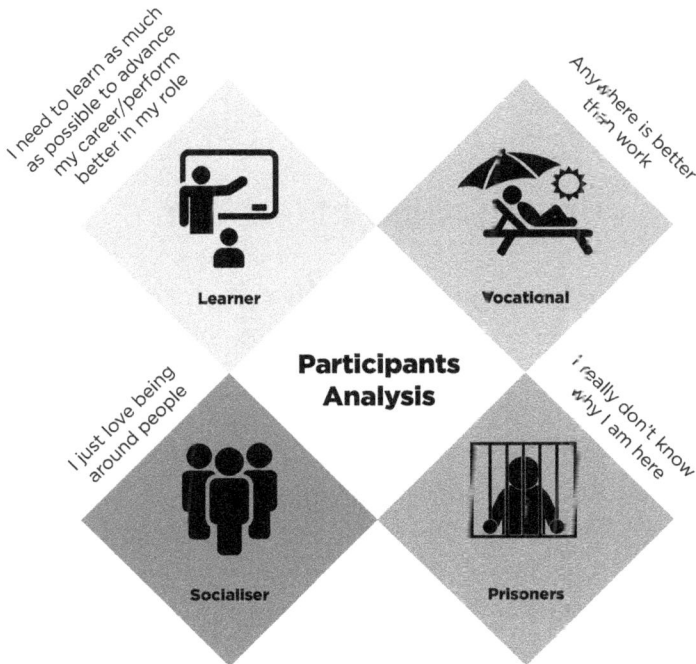

FIGURE 7: An interesting perspective of the various types of Adult Learners that might show up in your program

In summary, to overcome the barriers to adult learning, you need to have a good grasp of how to deliver your training so that it is:

i.   Relevant to the participant's personal or professional life.

ii. Organised in such a way as to promote the assimilation of new knowledge while linking up with established thoughts, experiences, knowledge, and expectations.

iii. Meaningful to the learner, i.e., they must be able to clearly identify what they will get from the training and how it will improve their life.

iv. Application-focused so that learning can be transferred from the classroom to the workplace or personal life.

"One day with a great teacher is better than a thousand days of diligent study."
Japanese Proverb

Instructional Methods

Once you have thoroughly studied and incorporated the principles of adult learning into your training delivery, the next step is to choose the right instructional methods. Some people erroneously believe that great content is all it takes to be successful as a Trainer. Even if your content is perfect, participants can easily disengage if the method used to share the information is incongruent with the objectives of the training. Imagine how you would feel if you attended a class to learn to how to fly fighter jets and it ended up being a day full of PowerPoint lectures.

Instructional methods generally fall into three categories: Trainer-centred, learner-centred, or a combination of both. Trainer-centred methods are best used when the Trainer is the subject matter expert and the participants know little to nothing about the subject. Learner-centred methods, on the other hand, are used when the participants have a lot of knowledge and experience about the subject matter. The method chosen should depend on the objectives of the training. Some objectives are best suited to Trainer-centred methods, while others need to be learner-centred.

Generally, Trainers should use a combination of instructional methods to ensure that all learners' needs are met. When varied instructional methods are used, learners benefit from a wide range of tools and would probably enjoy the session more. In choosing your instructional methods, take into account the fact that people learn differently and have unique learning styles. As a Trainer, you will find that there will rarely be a training session where everyone has the same learning style. So, your goal should be to incorporate as much variety as possible into your delivery to engage all learners and never completely alienate anyone. The four main learning styles are visual, auditory, kinaesthetic and intellectual.

Examples of Instructional Methods

TEACHER-CENTERED APPROACHES	TEACHER AND LEARNER COMBINATION APPROACHES	LEARNER-CENTERED APPROACHES
Lecture	Lecture with discussion	Case studies
Guest speaker	Video with discussion	Role plays
	Open and small group discussions	Brain storming/ panel of experts

Training Toolkit

Just like every craftsman needs to be properly equipped with the right toolkit, a professional Trainer is only as good as her tools. No matter how good you are as a presenter, if the microphone or speakers suddenly stop working while speaking to a large auditorium full of people, your outcomes will be affected. From marketing your services to delivering an outstanding training session, to meet the ever-changing needs of your customers effectively, you will require a range of tools. In this section, I recommend some of the top training tools that are invaluable in your work as a Trainer.

Profile or Bio

To make a great first impression, your profile must be clear, concise and customer centric.

Your profile is a professional introduction of you and your business. It essentially provides information about your services in the context of the market or customer you are serving. To make a great first impression, your profile must be clear, concise and customer centric. It should not just state that you are a Trainer. It should describe the problems you help customers solve through your training programs.

Brochures

Invest in professionally designed and printed brochures that lay out relevant details about your products and services in a compelling way.

Presentation Pitch Decks

The first formal opportunity you will probably get to demonstrate your competency and leave a lasting impression on potential clients will be when you pitch for the job brief. To demonstrate your expertise, you need to build presentation pitch decks that will convince potential clients of your ability to deliver an outstanding training beyond any reasonable doubt.

Your presentation decks should be created to educate the sponsor or management board. It should not just be a selling tool where you laud your business or drone on about your accomplishments and customer testimonials. While these should be included, you need to make the pitch about the customer and their needs. Prepare for the pitch as you would the actual training, and your objective should be to ensure they leave the room having learnt something new. Deliver your pitch so that the value potential customers gain from you becomes a benchmark that favours you when measured against your competitors.

Training Worksheets and Templates

People often equate learning, and erroneously so, with accumulating vast amounts of information. If participants leave a training session with just one piece of paper that lists the essential information or concepts from the training, it is quite likely they will feel dissatisfied.

Thick workbooks and bulging folders with papers spilling out are reminiscent of university days and bears an image of studiousness. But can you recollect how many of those course materials you actually studied cover to cover? Most likely the sheer bulk of it scared you and you ended up skimming the book for the most important information. Do not be tempted to confer the same burden on your learners. Create resource materials that are useful and will put the most essential information at their fingertips. These could be in the form of checklists, schematics of a technical process, diagrams, flowcharts, summary of key points, samples of pre-filled templates, frameworks, and models that learners can use on the job.

Video Resources

The very first YouTube video was uploaded on 23 April 2005. Today, three hundred hours of video content are uploaded to YouTube every minute! Stop to think this through for a minute. It really is quite illogical to not incorporate videos into your teaching experience.

Already, social media has dangerously reduced people's attention span. They now have access to so much information at the click of a button. In fact, they rarely need to pore through endless rows of sentences anymore (remember when the web was mainly text-based, and pictures were a rarity). All they need to do now is simply search for and watch the video on whatever it is they want to learn.

Having a good learning experience is first and foremost ensuring that training is learner-centred.

Videos have become too important to be ignored. Having a good learning experience is first and foremost ensuring that training is learner-centred. The majority of adult learners today use educational videos as a learning tool. Studies have shown that the use of short video clips stimulates the brain to process information efficiently and promote recall.

Previously, abstract topics and technical concepts that were very difficult to understand are now being taught effectively using videos. So, you really have no excuse for not incorporating videos into your training. Even if you are not ready to create your own videos, with permission, you can leverage videos created by others. There so many videos that have already been created – both free and at a cost. All you need to do is research the available options and select the right ones for your training. You may use the following questions as a guide when selecting videos for your training program:

- Does the video fit the purpose of the training program?

- Will the participants see it as relevant?

- Will the terminology and language used in the video be easily understood by your participants?

- Does the video contain information or concepts that can be easily applied? And are these suitable for the learner's competency level?

- Are the resources or materials used in the video readily available to help your participants follow along?

Videos can serve multiple purposes during a training program and should never be seen as a space-filler or used as a tactic to change the pace. Aside from using pre-recorded video clips, the training can also be recorded in real-time and used as a training tool later in the session. This is especially useful during skill-building exercises and practices, as it provides the participants with the opportunity to practise the skill, carry out self-appraisal, and receive feedback.

Various types of video-recording equipment are readily available for purchase depending on your budget and intended use. Make sure you research before investing your funds. Ideally, creation of training videos should be outsourced to a reliable contractor, so that you can focus on the core areas of your training business.

Graphics and Pictures

Pictures are worth a thousand words, but well-chosen images used at the right time are worth a million more. Presentation software that allows the use of images is widely popular nowadays, so it is easy to incorporate graphics and pictures into your training. Microsoft PowerPoint and Mac Keynote remain the most popular presentation software found on most computers and mobile devices. These allow you to create presentations that participants can access anytime, anywhere in the world.

As a Trainer, visual aids will also help you organise your thoughts, lessons, and teachings into a coherent flow, so that you can cover the key points of the training in a logical sequence.

Flip Charts

Flip charts can be hugely beneficial when creating visuals in real-time to support a concept or an idea you are passing across. But take heed, flip charts are widely misused. Do not be the Trainer who spends all day with his back turned to the participants, writing and drawing away. They are also quite

Do not be the Trainer who spends all day with his back turned to the participants, writing and drawing away.

unsuitable for training sessions with more than twenty participants.

Other Training Tools

Here are some of the other tools you should aim to build into your toolkit.

- Microphone (for virtual training/webinars)
- Database of case studies
- Evaluation/Feedback forms
- Attendance sheet
- Participation souvenirs
- Questionnaires
- Laptop
- Projector
- Slide mover
- Pre-course materials
- Administration Checklists
- Assessment tools

Visit **www.youmustbecomeatrainer.com** to download templates that can be included in your trainer toolkit.

Planning Your Training Session

The popular saying, "If you fail to plan, you plan to fail" holds absolutely true in the training profession. The need for thorough planning and preparation cannot be overemphasised. The following are four questions that if addressed competently will help you deliver the best possible training for your participants.

Who am I teaching?

As stated earlier, you must take time to know your audience before proceeding with any learning intervention. When you acquaint yourself with their demographics and their level of experience and familiarity with the content, you put yourself in a great position to devise the right training to meet their needs.

What am I teaching?

Take time to study and understand the content. Seek out subject matter experts that will help close any gaps in your knowledge. Get yourself to the point where you can answer participants' questions confidently and can also ask quality questions that will enhance their learning.

How will you teach it?

Create a strategy around how you will deliver the content, including the instructional methods and training activities you will use, and when. If you are unsure of how to create an appropriate delivery strategy, you could engage the services of a training course designer to help guide you.

How will I assess their learning?

You need to plan how you will assess the effectiveness of your training. Some key parameters you should assess are, how well participants acquired the new knowledge and skills, how well they applied them in solving problems, and how well their learning met the overarching goals of the training program. There are a number of ways to do this. For example, you could have them sit through an assessment both at the start and the end of the course to gauge their progression. Or, you could use application-style techniques such as case studies and role-plays during the training to identify how well they are utilising the knowledge in solving problems.

Of course, it is not enough to assess your participants. You should also give them feedback on their performance, and if possible, do so throughout the training. Feedback when used effectively can help boost the trainees' confidence and create a sense of satisfaction. Here are a few guidelines to note when giving feedback:

- Your primary goal should be to reinforce, motivate and encourage; not criticise.

- Try to sandwich constructive criticism with genuine praise.

- Make it clear that your feedback is an opinion and not a law that must be obeyed. Use words such as, "I can see you did ABC; I think if you do XYZ, you could get even better results."

- A rule of thumb is to never to give feedback in a way that you would not like to receive it.

Feedback when used effectively can help boost the trainees' confidence and create a sense of satisfaction.

Finally, before dismissing the class, ask participants to reflect on what they have learnt during the training and to create a simple action plan on how they intend to implement what they have learnt. This is very important if you want what they have learnt to stick and get applied. They can ask themselves questions like, what will I use the new knowledge, skills and attitudes to create? How will I do it? Who will hold me accountable until my action plan comes to fruition? How will I measure progress?

Keeping Participants Engaged and Motivated

The ARCS model created by John Keller is a great resource you can use to motivate participants during and after the training session. ARCS is an acronym that represents the four pillars of the model:

- Attention

- Relevance

- Confidence

- Satisfaction

Attention

This is all about getting your learners to be present and to actively show interest in discussions. Once adults become attentive, they become more willing to invest their time and energy into learning more about what has caught their attention. To stimulate interest during training, use the element of surprise by varying the tools and methods of instruction. Present intriguing data and facts and ask challenging questions to get them thinking. Tell stories to engage imagination; use humour to keep the atmosphere light and conducive for learning.

> *Once adults become attentive, they become more willing to invest their time and energy into learning more about what has caught their attention.*

Relevance

Do you recall Malcolm Knowles' principles of adult learning? Based on his findings, one of the assumptions a Trainer must make is, for adult learners to be engaged, the content must be relevant to them. They must know how the training content relates to their life and job performance. It is your job as the Trainer to make sure your messaging clearly relates to your audience's expectations. Do this by regularly highlighting how the training can be easily applied in their day to day life.

Confidence

The confidence level of learners often correlates with their motivation to learn and the effort they will invest in reaching their performance objectives. How can you boost learners' confidence? First, provide them with a clear roadmap for success. Confusion is one of the main reasons for loss of confidence. If learners have a step by step guide they can easily follow, they are more likely to feel confident in taking the necessary steps.

Second, affirm them by applauding their contributions and giving positive feedback throughout the session.

Confusion is one of the main reasons for loss of confidence.

Third, allow them the freedom to make their own learning decisions. Give time and space for learners to draw their conclusions and take ownership of their own learning.

Satisfaction

Learners need to derive some form of satisfaction from the learning experience if they are to stay committed to it. This could in the form of a personal sense of achievement from completing a part of the training or receiving praise from the Trainer. When learners can see and appreciate the results they are getting, they are more likely to stay focused.

To keep their satisfaction level high, the training should be designed in such a way that it allows them to get quick wins by using their newly learned skills as soon as possible. A note of caution here, however. Avoid over-rewarding participants as this could backfire and cause resistance if they feel the praise is undeserved and patronising.

ARCS MODEL UTILIZATION CHART			
Attention	**Relevance**	**Confidence**	**Satisfaction**
Perceptual Arousal Provide novelty and surprise	**Goal Orientation** Present objectives and useful purpose of instruction and specific methods for successful achievement	**Learning Requirements** Inform students about learning and performance requirements and assessment criteria	**Intrinsic Reinforcement** Encourage and supposrt intrinsic enjoyment of the learning experience
Inquiry Arousal Stimulate curiosity by posing questions or problems to solve	**Motive Matching** Match objectives to students needs and motives	**Successful Opportunities** Provide challenging and meaningful opportunities for successful learning	**Extrinsic Rewards** Provide positive reinforcement and motivational feedback
Variability Incorporate a range of methods and media to meet students' varying needs	**Familiarity** Present content in ways that are understandable and relate to the learners' experiences and values	**Personal Responsibility** Link learning success to students personal effort and ability	**Equity** Maintain consistent standards and consequences for success

Managing the Training Time

Always remember that time is a precious and limited resource, not just for you but for your learners as well. The quickest way for a learner to disengage from a training is if they feel their time is being wasted. When you carry on about a topic that has since lost the interest of the class, you are indirectly showing that you do not value their time. If participants get bored and switch off, it becomes difficult for them to retain key knowledge from the training.

As a Trainer, you must continually work on your time management. Never take it for granted that learners will stay in the room until you have finished delivering all the content planned. Poor time management can create stress. An executive who has to catch a flight after the training, for example, or a mother who has to pick up her child from school would quickly become anxious and stressed if the training overran. A good assumption to make is, once the time allocated for the training is up, you lose approximately half of the class. That will keep you mindful of how you apportion time as you work to cover all the objectives.

> *The quickest way for a learner to disengage from a training is if they feel their time is being wasted.*

At the start of each session, provide the class with an agenda that clearly shows how time will be spent. This will keep your participants from becoming anxious or stressed about time and will also keep you on track. Depending on the nature of the training, you could also task one or more of the participants with keeping you and the class accountable to the prescribed schedule.

Managing Difficult Participants

One of the main challenges you will face as a facilitator is dealing with participants who present attitudes and actions that make it difficult for others to learn or for the session to flow as planned. These attitudes could be in the form of talkativeness, venting, being argumentative or self-opinionated, creating distractions with pointless jokes and side conversations, or monopolising the Trainer's time and attention. Fortunately, there are many ways you can prevent or overcome these issues.

Arguably, the most effective strategy is to explicitly lay out the ground rules at the start of the training and help everyone in the room reach some form of agreement. You can take this even further by helping them take individual and joint responsibility for the success of the process. This should be done in a non-threatening way, and if possible, participants should be given the opportunity to come up with some of the rules themselves.

Also, acknowledge and empathise with some of the difficulties that participants may have faced in order to attend. Were they forced to attend because it is company policy? Is the training a last desperate attempt to boost their performance before they are sacked? It is worth recognising these issues and helping them to realise that whether they are there by choice or coercion, they still have the power to ensure they gain value from the experience. By addressing the issue and not shying away from it, you prevent it from causing problems later in the training.

And finally, as emphasised repeatedly in this chapter, create an atmosphere that engages participants positively right from the start. Welcome them individually and try to have a conversation with each participant. Actively draw them into discussions early on, rather than simply talking at them in a traditional student-teacher way. The more participants engage in discussions and activities, the more they feel responsible for the success of the training process and their own learning.

Key Takeaways

- To deliver the best outcomes for learners, a Trainer must pay close attention to the content of a training, as well as how it is delivered. No matter how exceptional the content is, its impact will be severely limited if the audience does not receive or understand it.

- An exceptional Trainer does not just instruct; he provokes learning by inspiring participants to engage fully with the content, to do their best thinking during the training and to take definite steps in applying the new information or skill.

- The best trainings are the ones where the content and delivery have been expertly matched to the audience, and a variety of instructional methods, tools and resources are deployed to cater for their individual needs.

- In summary, to become an exceptional Trainer, you must study your audience extensively, design the training to address their context skilfully, choose the right tools, manage the training time and space efficiently and be adept at inspiring the audience to take relevant action.

PART 3

START MAKING MONEY AS A TRAINER

Monetise your expertise by creating and capturing value

9

YOU MUST CREATE A SUSTAINABLE BUSINESS MODEL

"Understanding a business model requires not only knowing the compositional elements, but also grasping the interdependencies between elements. This is easier to express visually than through words. This is even more true when several elements and relationships are involved."
Alexander Osterwalder,

As you have learned in this book so far, jumping onto the training or course creator bandwagon without properly equipping yourself with the right knowledge, tools and know-how could mean a catastrophically short-lived training career or business. Like any business or career venture, it is best to create a solid plan before taking a major step forward.

Choosing your training pathway

One of the most important decisions you must make during your preparation season is how you intend to generate income as a Trainer. While there is no shortage of opportunities for Trainers, essentially, you will either work as a professional Trainer within an organisation or as a business owner who delivers training programs to individuals or organisations. If you choose the entrepreneurial path, you will need to acquire clients to generate revenue for your business. Whereas, as a professional Trainer, you will need to find a company that will employ you and pay you a salary.

Working as a Trainer within a corporate organisation

One of the most apparent benefits of working for an organisation is a steady stream of income, since in-house positions are typically salaried roles that come with benefits and bonuses. Another unique advantage of working in-house is that you are immersed in the business and therefore are able to gain an intimate knowledge of the company and its organisational goals. You will also get to see the results of your training efforts over time, as opposed to if you trained groups from various organisations on a one-off basis. Seeing the results of your training in this way can help you fine-tune and streamline your content.

The downside though is, there may be little flexibility in your schedule. You will likely work a set number of hours like a typical employee. Your earning potential may also be capped unless you work for a company that offers performance bonuses. Lastly, since there will be less variation in the training required within the organisation, it might get boring for you after a while. But working in-house could be a good option if the company brand is one that resonates with you and your values.

Working as a freelancer for a training agency

Most training agencies are business-to-business (B2B) organisations that either operate across a wide range of industries or are targeted at a particular niche. As a freelancer working for a training agency, you will not need to worry about marketing your business and finding clients. The downside however is, you will not get to choose who you work with.

Depending on the agency, you might work full-time hours or on a contractual basis. You might be deployed to the client's workplace to train, or work from a centralised location secured by the agency as part of the client's fee. You might also train remotely via conference calls or online workshops.

You may be given the training materials or expected to create them yourself. You may be required to abide by certain processes and policies. This can be seen as either an advantage or a disadvantage depending on how much control you want to have over your content and instructional methods. Similar to working in-house for a corporate organisation, your earning potential may also be capped.

Establishing a training business

As a business owner, you get to set your own rates and be your own boss. Most likely, you will start as a solo act until you have enough clients to outsource the other aspects of your business. This means that in the early stages of your business, you will wear many hats and not just be the Trainer! To be successful in business, you will need to have in place a viable plan for managing your finances, marketing your services, and carrying out essential administrative tasks. You also need to get a handle on your own taxes, either by learning proper accounting processes or by hiring a tax consultant.

This means that in the early stages of your business, you will wear many hats and not just be the Trainer!

Since you are not employed by a corporation, you can charge a higher rate for your services, but keep in mind that your fees need to cover all the additional costs that come with being self-employed, and later on an employer as your business grows. But the reality is that most new businesses fail within the first two years. This is not a statistic that is meant to scare you away but to emphasise that growing a business is not for the faint hearted. However, if you are committed to making it work, establishing a training business can be quite advantageous.

Clearly, all three options have their own advantages and disadvantages. What will work best for you will depend on your personal desires, professional goals, and chosen niche. Here are a few questions you can ask yourself to determine the best path for you:

1. Do you prefer to train online, in-person, or both?

2. How much flexibility do you need in your work schedule?

3. Are you comfortable with fluctuating income?

4. Are you comfortable with the extra responsibility that comes with running a business?

5. How much control do you want over how your training content is developed and delivered?

There are no right or wrong answers to these questions. They are simply designed to get you thinking about how each training pathway could impact your career and lifestyle. It is very important to note that just because you choose one path does not mean you cannot change later. In fact, many Trainers start off by working in-house or for an agency so that they can acquire the experience and skills that would help them find early success when they launch their own business.

"Entrepreneurs don't usually fail from circumstance; they fail from what I call entrepreneurial rigidity—a fixed mindset and unwillingness to change the business model."
Richie Norton

Creating your business model

Once you have decided on your income pathway, the next step is to create an operating model that will position you for success in your training business or career. You have to develop a profile of the program you plan to run and carry out extensive research on the organisations you want to target. To do that effectively, I highly recommend using the Business Model Canvas. It can be applied whether you are building a training business or career.

A Business Model Canvas is a simple one-page document that clearly states what you want to do in your business and how you will go about doing it. It allows you to plan your business strategy and brainstorm potential challenges you may face along the way. Boiled down to the nitty gritty, the Business Model Canvas is a set of nine powerful questions that if answered thoroughly will set your business up on the right foundation.

Business Model Canvas

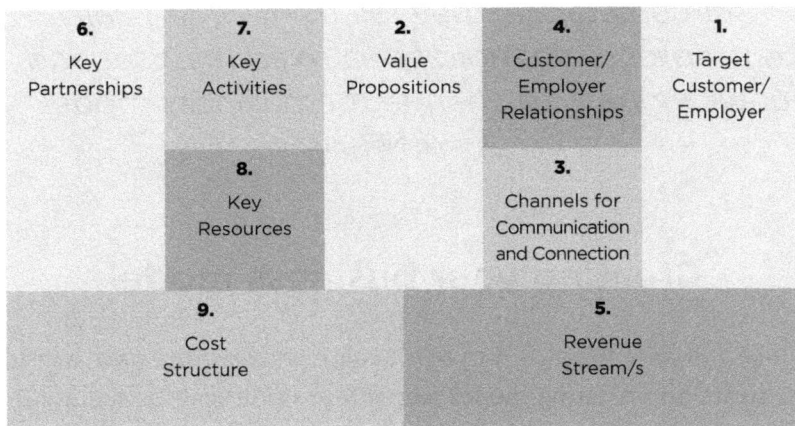

6.	7.	2.	4.	1.
Key Partnerships	Key Activities	Value Propositions	Customer/ Employer Relationships	Target Customer/ Employer
	8.		3.	
	Key Resources		Channels for Communication and Connection	
9.			5.	
Cost Structure			Revenue Stream/s	

The first question is about your customer. Who is the ideal customer that you will be targeting with your business? If it is a career you are trying to build, who are the ideal employers you are looking to work with? I cannot over-emphasise the importance of targeting the right customers who will resonate with what you are offering. You must know their needs, the challenges they are facing and the solutions they are searching for.

As a Trainer looking to build a business, you must determine if your customers are in a mass market or a niche market. If you are targeting corporate organisations, you must be able to describe the ideal company size and the titles, roles, and duties of the people who would be engaging your service. Likewise, you need to decide if you will be focused on a particular subset of an organisation, or if you will offer your services to a more diverse clientele.

After identifying who the customer is, the next question is, what value are you offering them? What are you bringing to the table? What's in it for them? What will you promise in return for their payment? What problem will you help them solve? What needs will you help them meet? How does your proposed value address the customer's problem? What incremental value should they expect from working with you instead of your competitors? What value are your competitors offering, and how can you offer better value? How accessible, convenient, and usable will this value be for the customer? The value you offer could be financial or non-financial, depending on how you choose to meet your customer's needs. As you answer these questions, note that there must be a strong alignment between your targeted customer and the value you are offering. For example, if you are targeting commercial banks, offering them a training on the latest breakthroughs in cancer treatment is unlikely to be considered valuable.

The third question helps you define the channels of communication between you and your customer. How will you connect or communicate with your target customers? What resources are available? Which ones work best? Which are the most cost-effective? What tools will you use to draw attention to your business' value proposition? What channels will you use to deliver the proposed offer? You need to make it easy for your customers to purchase your services.

The fourth relates to customer relations. How will you build, maintain, and sustain your relationship with customers? More importantly, what type of relationship will each customer expect you to maintain with them? How will these relationships integrate with the rest of your operating model? How will you continue to foster the connection between your business and your customer after they have engaged your services? It is crucial for you to capture the strategy you will adopt to create and maintain the right relationship with your customers.

Next, you focus on revenue. How will you make money? If it is a career path, how will you make money apart from your salary? Will you negotiate to receive bonuses for outstanding results? If it is a business venture, you need to plan how you will generate revenue. What training are your target customers willing to pay for? How much are they willing to pay? What will be your revenue model? Will you be charging per head or per class? How many customers will it require to create a sustainable revenue stream? What would be the average contract or transaction value?

The sixth question leads you to identify the key partners you need to collaborate with. As a Trainer, you may need to partner with organisations, for example, that own training facilities you want to hire. You may also need to partner with other Trainers to deliver a well-rounded training experience. Think through and identify who these partners are and how you will manage your relationship with them.

The seventh step gets you thinking about the essential activities you will carry out as a Trainer. What activities will you do daily, weekly, and monthly to ensure you deliver value to your customers? What are the activities that support your customer communication channels, your partnerships and of course, your revenue stream?

The eighth question drives you to identify the key competencies and resources you should acquire to deliver your value proposition. What are the skills you really need to be excellent at? What sorts of resources do you need to excel as a Trainer?

And finally, what will it cost to deliver the value proposition? How much will it cost to carry out key activities, work with partners, and build the required capability to succeed? Which key activities and resources are the most expensive? What is the most appropriate cost structure you can adopt to deliver your proposed value? Have you identified your fixed and variable costs? Will your business be cost-driven or value-driven? If you are looking at a career as a Trainer in a corporate organisation, what will it cost you to become your targeted employer's preferred candidate?

Let us apply the Business Canvas in practice. Say you have decided to focus on the Train-The-Trainer (TTT) niche, and you have gained the right knowledge and skills through professional courses and certification. You have researched your competitors and identified two target customers: corporate organisations with in-house Trainers and freelance Trainers. Both target customers must have their own specific value proposition prepared for them in a way that uniquely addresses their needs. The large organisations want to do more with less and are looking for ways to reduce their training costs. Whereas, freelance trainers are looking to monetise their expertise.

Next, you consider the channels of communication you will use to connect with them. Your options might include pitching your proposals via video conferencing software such as Zoom, or through emails, phone calls, or face to face meetings.

Following that, you decide how you will generate revenue. You could charge per head or per class of fifteen, for example. You would need to design a unique revenue stream generator for each customer segment.

> *You would need to design a unique revenue stream generator for each customer segment.*

Who are the key partners you need to create the TTT program? You may need a printing company for the training manuals and workbooks. You may need to hire training facilities like *TheZone.ng* to run your training in a conducive environment. If you choose to run the TTT training program franchise, you would need to register with the accrediting organisation and get certified by them.

What key competencies do you need? At the very least, you need an in-depth knowledge of the TTT curriculum, along with good presentation and communication skills.

What key activities do you need to carry out? There are several, including developing your proposal, creating the training content and hiring an assistant to help with some of the administrative tasks.

What are the associated costs? This is an ever-growing list! Everything listed above will cost you money. In addition, you will need to invest in training tools such as projectors.

By duly and diligently answering all nine questions in the Business Model Canvas, you can create an effective blueprint for your training business or career. See below a pre-filled sample of the Business Model Canvas for a training business. Visit **www.youmustbecomeatrainer. com** to download a blank editable template.

TRAINING BUSINESS MODEL

KEY ACTIVITIES:	STRATEGIC ALLIANCES/ PARTNERSHIPS:	VALUE PROPOSITION:	CUSTOMER RELATIONSHIPS:	CUSTOMER SEGMENTS:
• Research & advisory • Teaching • Publishing • Pitching presentations • Instructional design & content creation • Curriculum design • Conference & events • Faculty curation, sourcing & management • Community engagement & management • Partner acquisition and management • Sales and business development • Marketing • Admin/Execution • Facility management • Proposal & report writing • Industry breakfast meeting • PR and communications managment • CSR	• Certification, curriculum & accreditation partners • Facilitators & SME/ Practitioners • CSR sponsors • Professional associations/bodies • Caterers, printers & other vendors • Research firms • Marketing & PR firms • African based learning providers	• Industry focused content • Research based • SME/Practitioner driven • Rockstar faculty • Problem solving/ application focused • Market led/outside-in • Technology enabled • Career enhancement • Conducive learning environment • Networking	• Learning advisory • Community of practice • Collaboration/ co-creation • Leveraging studio as a platform • Key account managment • Alumni events • Knowledgement sharing session • CRM	• Professionals • Corporate organisations • Entrepreneurs • Facilitators/practitioners • Social enterprises • Public sector • African-based learning providers
	KEY RESOURCES/ COMPETENCIES: • Facility • Faculty • Funding • Human resources • Intellectual property • Technology • Playbook • Research		**CHANNELS:** • Thought leadership • Journals, books & publications • Videos, app store, website, webinars & blogs • Testimonials • Digital marketing • Direct sales/marketing • Online learning platform	

COST:
• Human resources • Research • Curriculum & certifications
• Faculty • Admin & logistics • Technology • PR & marketing
• Facility management • Printing/stationaries

REVENUE:
• Enrolment fees • Grants from partners
• Digital content sale/subscription • Programme value management
• Revenue from African based partners • Research

Key Takeaways

- There are three main ways to generate income in training: as a Trainer employed within a corporate organisation, as a freelancer for a training agency, or by establishing a training business.

- As a Trainer within a corporate organisation, you would have access to a steady income (plus the possibility of bonuses and other benefits). Disadvantages could be lack of flexibility in your working hours and choice of training content, capped earning potential and boredom from delivering the same training repeatedly.

- Similar to the employed Trainer, as a freelancer for a training agency you would earn your pay by training on behalf of an established organisation. The downside is, you are also likely to have very little input into important elements of the training such as content, instructional methods, choice of clients etc.

- As a business owner, you are your own boss and can set the direction of the business. You have the flexibility to choose what and who you train. Your earning potential is also uncapped. However, you would be responsible for all aspects of the business including marketing and acquisition of clients. Running a successful business requires a lot of hard work, dedication and grit. It is not for the faint-hearted.

- A Business Model Canvas is a simple one-page document that showcases your business strategy and clearly states what you want to do in your business and how you will go about doing it. To create a business canvas, you answer nine powerful questions that will guide your decision-making and set your business on the right foundation.

YOU **MUST** BECOME A **TRAINER**

10

YOU MUST BECOME
A MARKETER

"The company with the best marketing wins."
Ryan Deiss

With the benefit of hindsight, if I had the opportunity to start my training business all over again, I would prioritise marketing above everything else.

"Everything else?" You might ask. "Isn't that a bit radical?"

It may sound a bit over the top, but in my twenty-year entrepreneurial journey, I have learnt over and over again that marketing is the lifeblood of a business. For any business to succeed, it must prioritise marketing above product development, operations, human resources, and everything else. Marketing when done right leads to sales, and without sales, you do not have a business.

If you get nothing else out of this book, you must get this – marketing is the biggest determining factor of success in career or business, regardless of your industry. You cannot afford to treat marketing as an afterthought. It much be front and centre of your business strategy.

Unfortunately, this is counterintuitive for business owners. The typical entrepreneur is passionate about their product, which is understandable because the product is what inspired them to start the business in the first place. They fall madly in love with their product and all their money and attention are spent on it. They keep testing it, tweaking it and improving it, believing that as long as they have a great product people will flock in to buy. Falling in love with your product is a grave mistake. You end up spending a disproportionate amount of time and resources focusing on your product and ignoring the only reason you are in business – the market. This is a common problem in entrepreneurship.

...marketing is the biggest determining factor of success in career or business, regardless of your industry.

LinkedIn co-founder, Reid Hoffman said, "If you are not embarrassed by the first version of your product, you've launched too late." And by that he meant, let the market decide what is great and what is not. Do not give in to the temptation to sit on your product, pruning and perfecting it based only on your own ideas. By prioritising marketing, you will constantly draw the attention of the market to your product and that gives you the fantastic opportunity to mould it into exactly what your target customers want.

Hoffman went on to say, "Many entrepreneurs still identify so closely with their products or services they cannot bring themselves to adopt a mindset that prioritises iteration and learning over perfection. As an entrepreneur, you often base your whole sense of identity and self-worth on your 'baby' – and that almost guarantees a sense of driven perfectionism. You believe that you are going to be judged on your product – or even equated with it – so you want everything to be exactly right upon the initial unveiling."

The harsh reality is, no matter how great your product is, if the right people do not hear about it and become convinced of its value enough to buy it, your product will continue to gather dust on the shelves and it would not be long before your business folds up. The company with the best product does not win in the marketplace; the company with the best marketing does.

What is Marketing?

There are two definitions of marketing that I really love. The first is by Philip Kotler, popularly known as the Father of Modern Marketing. He defined marketing as the science and art of exploring, creating, and delivering value to satisfy the needs of a target market at a profit. According to Kotler, marketing occurs in four stages. One, it identifies the market's unfulfilled needs and desires. Two, it defines, measures and quantifies the size of the identified market and the profit potential. Three, it pinpoints which segment of the organisation can best serve that need. And four, it designs and promotes the appropriate products and services.

The second definition of marketing is by Allan Dib, author of 1-Page marketing. He said: "If the circus is coming to town and you paint a sign saying, 'Circus Coming to the Showgrounds Saturday,' that's advertising. If you put the sign on the back of an elephant and walk it into town, that's promotion. If the elephant walks through the mayor's flower bed and the local newspaper writes a story about it, that's publicity. And if you get the mayor to laugh about it, that's public relations. If the town's citizens go to the circus, you show them the many entertainment booths, explain how much fun they'll have spending money at the booths, answer their questions, and ultimately, they spend a lot at the circus, that's sales. And if you planned the whole thing, that's marketing!"

Alan Dib's definition brilliantly illustrates that marketing goes way beyond advertising. Many businesses equate marketing with advertising. Once they have put out a few adverts, they think their marketing is done. Running adverts is only one component of the marketing process. Marketing is an intricate cycle of creative ideas, tactics and actions that requires careful and intelligent planning.

> *Marketing is an intricate cycle of creative ideas, tactics and actions that requires careful and intelligent planning.*

"At its very core, marketing is storytelling. The best advertising campaigns take us on an emotional journey — appealing to our wants, needs, and desires — while at the same time telling us about a product or service."

Melinda Partin

Creating Your Strategic Marketing Plan

The key to successfully marketing your training business begins with developing a strategic marketing plan that is designed to help you achieve your business goals. It should clearly lay out the different levels of marketing activities you will engage in based on specific business targets and research. And of course, it will also require diligent execution of that plan. There is no profit in creating an elaborate marketing strategy and then defaulting to old habits when pressure mounts and other areas of the business take priority over marketing. Your marketing plan should be reviewed regularly to ensure it is implemented in a timely manner.

I wish I had a guide like this book when I started out on my journey as a Trainer, almost twenty years ago. It would have made a phenomenal difference to my business growth. That is why I am making it available to you. In the rest of this chapter, I will use a case study to walk you through the eight major steps of an effective marketing strategy so that you can competently market your training services and achieve your business or career goals.

My case study is centred on Elizabeth, who has ten years' experience as a full-time sales professional in the financial services industry. She absolutely loves sales and has been very successful at it, earning several promotions and bonuses during her career. She is confident that she can create a successful business by training sales professionals in the financial services sector to multiply their sales.

The first investment Elizabeth made into her business was to obtain a professional training certification. Naturally, the next goal on her agenda was to start attracting clients and generating income. The following steps lay out in detail how a new business can become profitable in a short amount of time.

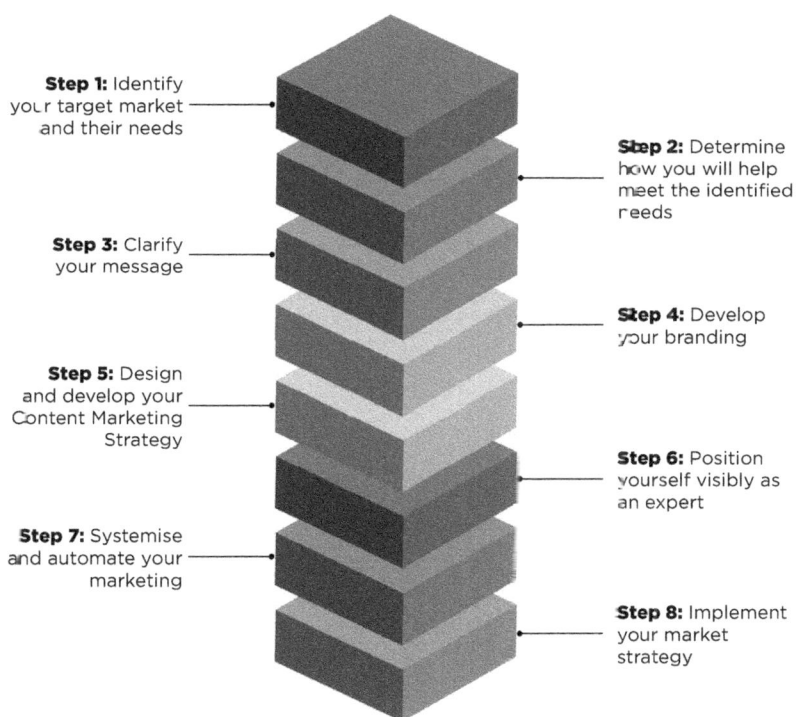

Step 1: Identify your target market and their needs

Step 2: Determine how you will help meet the identified needs

Step 3: Clarify your message

Step 4: Develop your branding

Step 5: Design and develop your Content Marketing Strategy

Step 6: Position yourself visibly as an expert

Step 7: Systemise and automate your marketing

Step 8: Implement your market strategy

FIGURE 8: How a new business can become profitable in a short amount of time

Step 1 – Identify your target market and their most crucial needs

This is the first and most important step. Elizabeth did not leave this to chance. Neither did she make assumptions about what her potential clients need, even though she had vast experience in that industry. She invested time and money into thoroughly researching her target market and identified the following:

- There were approximately two hundred financial services organisations that fell within her target market.

- Of all the needs those organisations faced, the most urgent and pervasive need they were willing to pay for was transitioning their sales force from transactional sellers into trusted financial advisors.

- Fifteen of the organisations indicated a willingness to buy from her immediately if she could create a customised workshop that would help them improve considerably in that area. This was clearly a huge business opportunity for Elizabeth considering the number of sales personnel within each of those organisations ranged from 100 to 250.

Step 2 – Determine how you will help meet their identified needs

Next, Elizabeth carried out a SWOT analysis to thoroughly assess her capabilities and how well she could meet the needs identified by her target market. These were her findings.

Strengths

- Subject Matter Expertise: Elizabeth is a financial services sales expert with a track record of several outstanding successes.

- Industry Experience: She has extensive sales experience as a trusted advisor in the financial services sector.

- Professional Training Certification: By completing a Train-the-Trainer certification course, Elizabeth has gained the relevant knowledge and tools to successfully deliver the training.

- Training Experience: She has facilitated several trainings as an in-house Trainer.

Weaknesses

- Limited Capacity: As a solo Trainer, Elizabeth is likely to face many challenges in running multiple trainings for different organisations.

- Limited Marketing Experience: Although Elizabeth has many years of sales experience, her exposure to the marketing side of the business is limited.

Opportunities

- Expert Knowledge: Elizabeth's in-depth knowledge of the role and the industry is a major advantage.

- Professional Certification: Her Train-the-Trainer certification from a renowned institution adds a layer of credibility to her business and gives her an edge over competitors who are not professionally trained.

Threats

- Competition: As a solopreneur just starting out, she will face fierce competition from bigger and more established training companies.

- Testimonials: She has no documented record of executing training programs on this scale.

Visit **www.youmustbecomeatrainer.com** to download a copy of the SWOT framework for your use.

Strengths	Weaknesses	Opportunities	Threats
• Subject Matter Expertise: • Real hands-on field experience in the area of selling as a trusted advisor • Professional Training Certification: • Previous experience running similar training	• Capacity considering the size of the project • Limited Marketing experience/ resources	• In-depth knowledge of the role and industry. • Professionala trainer status	• Bigger and more established Training Company • Inability to show track record of executing similar projects successfully

Based on the results of her SWOT analysis, Elizabeth developed the following strategies:

- She would increase her capacity to meet the demands of large-scale training projects by collaborating with other competent Trainers.

- She would leverage other people's track records by purchasing a training franchise from a well-established company with years of experience and proven results.

- She would offer to run a free pilot program for the organisations to showcase what she had to offer.

- She would work with marketing consultants to develop a robust marketing strategy for her business.

Step 3 – Clarify your message

Next, Elizabeth set out to become crystal clear about her messaging. She understood that for prospective clients to engage her services, she had to learn to speak their language. She had to use words that would clearly identify their most pressing needs and spell out how she would help meet those needs. She knew this was absolutely critical to her success, so she conducted extensive research on the internet to find resources that could guide her through the process of clarifying her message. She came across *StoryBrand*, one of the most effective frameworks organisations can use to clarify their marketing message. Using the framework, she refined the promotional offer for her training program and finally settled on this concise but powerful statement below:

At ActiveLearning, we understand your drive to become the go-to firm for your target customers. We also understand that to do this, you need to be best-in-class at attracting, retaining, and growing your customer base. The challenge, however, is that your salespeople are struggling to engage and win key customer accounts. You feel deeply frustrated that you are losing potential clients to competitors in the marketplace.

With the right training and tools, we believe your sales results and performance can significantly improve. We can help your organisation increase its sales performance by transitioning your sales force into trusted advisors that customers are eager to do business with. And this is exactly what we will do:

i.   We will deep-dive and gain an in-depth understanding of your business context.

ii. We will design and deliver training programs customised to the context of your organisation.

iii. We will measure and track the performance of your salespeople to ensure they successfully transition to trusted advisors.

Schedule your free consultation today. We look forward to discussing how we can help move your business forward.

Step 4 – Branding

Branding is how people perceive your company. Usually, it is their first contact with your company and will likely influence their first impression of you and your services. Consequently, branding should by no means be trivialised. Elizabeth engaged the services of a freelance graphics designer to create the visual elements of her branding including the logo, website, business cards and other marketing stationery. She did not want a website that would sit pretty and do nothing. She wanted a website that would consistently generate quality leads for her business and help convert them into paying customers. She benchmarked several websites and worked with her web designer until the structure, functionality, and presentation of her website was perfectly aligned with her business goals. Visit **www.**

youmustbecomeatrainer.com/trustedadvisor to see a copy of the website and to watch a video walkthrough of the site.

Step 5 – Design your Content Marketing Strategy (CMS)

Traditional or direct marketing methods such as flyers, billboards, and television, radio and newspaper advertisements have seen a major decline in popularity and conversion rates over the last few years. Many consumers have grown tired of hearing the same old sales pitches. More so, with the advent of digitalisation and the public's unprecedented access to information, consumers are no longer taking marketers' claims at face value. The consumer is now more likely to research and compare products and services extensively before making a purchase.

If you want to get ahead of the competition, you have to learn quickly how to earn the trust of your customers. The most effective way to do this is to educate your target market by sharing valuable content and relevant information that will help them make good buying decisions. If they learn to trust the information you are supplying, when they decide to buy, you will be their first choice. This approach to marketing is called Education-Based Marketing, or Content Marketing.

If you want to get ahead of the competition, you have to learn quickly how to earn the trust of your customers.

Based on her research into the target market, Elizabeth adopted Content Marketing as her primary marketing strategy. She then identified ten proven tactics she would use as part of her Content Marketing strategy. These include:

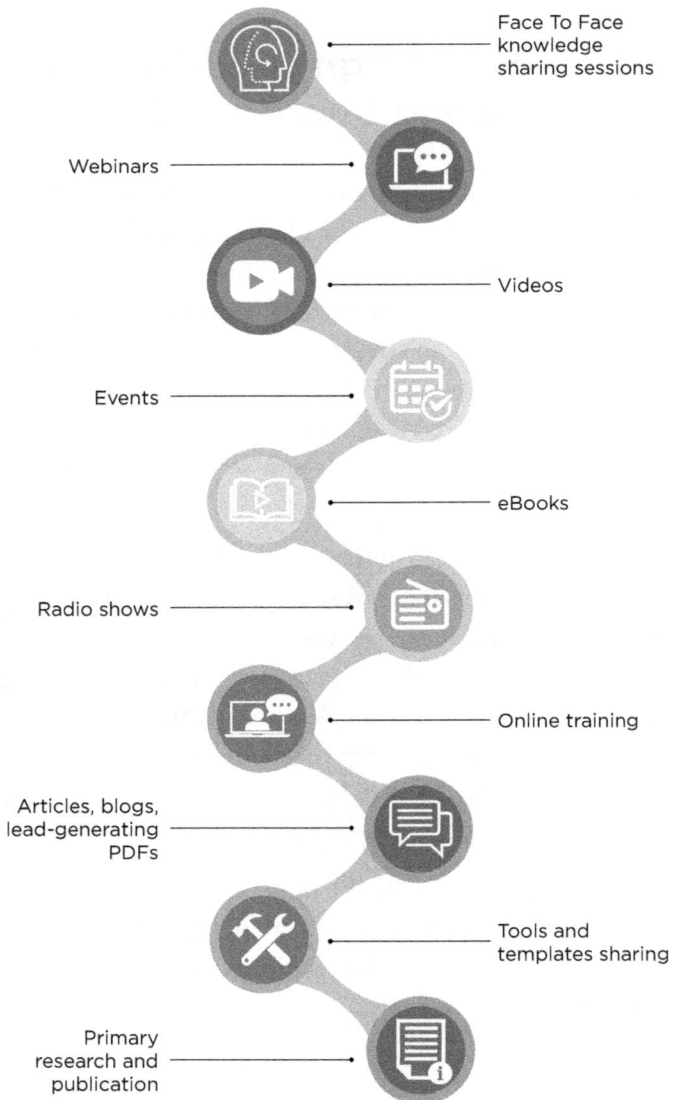

FIGURE 10: 10 Content Marketing Strategy

Step 6 – Position yourself as an expert

One of the challenges you will face when venturing into a new business or career is "Pre-Framing", which is a business term for how people will view you or your business before they have engaged with you long enough to form a proper judgment. If you show up as a newbie with no experience or track record of success, they are likely to pre-frame you as incompetent and therefore, a risky investment.

How, then, do you command the attention of your target audience and convince them you can deliver what you are promising when you do not have a long list of testimonials or referrals that speak for you? You can scale this hurdle of a lack of trust by visibly positioning yourself as an expert in your niche and sharing expert industry knowledge that your market finds valuable.

If you can successfully position yourself as a knowledgeable expert in your niche, you will create a solid avenue for your target audience to pre-frame you as an expert who can be trusted. And fortunately, digitalisation has made this considerably easy to do. There are many high performing content marketing tools you can use to build trust with your ideal customers including blogs, eBooks, webinars, case studies, social media posts, podcasts, videos, public speaking, articles, and infographics.

To position herself as the go-to trainer in the financial services sales space, Elizabeth chose to publish an information guide to educate her target customers on the main differences between a transactional sales professional and a trusted advisor, and why every organisation should invest in transforming their sales force into trusted advisors. By publishing this guide, she would be educating her target customers, whilst positioning herself as the most suitable provider to meet that need.

Creating a Lead-Generating PDF Guide

To create the guide, Elizabeth thoroughly researched the topic and interlaced her findings with her vast experience in sales advisory to write a report on the top seven differences between transactional sales professionals and trusted advisors. She also presented a strong case for organisations to make the transition urgently with research-backed arguments. She distilled this information into a concise but punchy guide that busy executives could consume in very little time and more importantly, could easily implement in their organisations for a quick win. Lastly, she hosted the PDF on her website and directed potential clients there to download free of charge in exchange for their contact details – primarily their first name and email address. Visit **www. youmustbecomeatrainer.com/trustedadvisor** to download a copy of the Lead Generating PDF.

Step 7 – Systemise and automate your marketing

Now that her PDF guide was set up to generate potential customer leads round the clock, the next step in her marketing strategy was to create an automated email campaign to nurture those leads and convert them into paying customers. It was not enough to collect email addresses; she had to continue to nurture those connections and keep herself firmly in their mind by sending regular emails packed with valuable content. For this to work, she discovered that the emails had to be automated. By automating her email sequences, she could schedule the emails in advance and optimise them to be sent at times when the customer was most likely to open and engage with them. This would be virtually impossible to do manually, with her email list growing rapidly and already starting to attract international leads who live in different time zones.

Sample Email Nurture Campaign

Email 1

Subject Line: *Here's Your Guide: 7 Key Attributes of a Successful Trusted Advisor*

Hi <insert name>,

Here's the free guide you requested: 7 Key Attributes of a Successful Trusted Advisor.

If you are losing sales because your salespeople are acting like order-takers and not trusted advisors, then you want to download this right away.

[Download Now]

After reviewing the guide, you'll understand the importance of making the transition to trusted advisor and the main challenges that are preventing sales professionals from making that change. You'll also be encouraged to know that transitioning your team of salespeople from order-takers to trusted advisors is easier than you think.

This guide will walk you through the process.

[Download Now]

Kind Regards,

<insert name>

Email 2

Subject Line: *The Secret to Winning More Business*

Hi <insert name>,

Your customers have problems they're trying to solve. But they are so close to their businesses, they often can't see what to do next. That's where you come in.

Are you helping them solve their problems? Are you proactively identifying solutions to their biggest pain points? Or, is your sales team merely taking their orders?

The key to winning more business is to be a trusted advisor to your customers.

Trusted advisors have a deep understanding of their customer's business, and they apply this knowledge in helping them win more business.

They educate their clients by sharing relevant knowledge and insights. They are effective in helping them see around the corner and prepare for the unknown.

Because they demonstrate strong business and financial acumen, they become the go-to advisors on crucial financial and business matters.

If you can transition your salespeople from order-takers into trusted advisors, you will win more business.

For more information on how to make the transition, visit <insert page link>

Kind Regards,

<insert name>

Email 3

Subject Line: *Beating the Competition Is Easier Than You Think*

Hi <insert name>,

Winning new business can be difficult. It's especially frustrating if your competition is cutting prices to win more deals.

But your customers aren't always looking for the lowest price. They are looking for the best value. When you help your customers solve their problems, you are giving them value.

Helping them solve problems requires a deep understanding of their business. That takes time and effort. Most competitors are not willing to do what it takes to truly understand their customer's business.

If your salespeople are willing to understand your customers' problems and become their trusted advisors, you will beat the competition.

At ActiveLearning, we offer a training program to help your sales team make the transition to trusted advisors and therefore, beat the competition.

Get ahead of your competition and get started today. Find out more here: <insert page link>

Kind Regards,

<insert name>

Email 4

Subject Line: *The #1 Thing Salespeople Get Wrong*

Hi <insert name>,

The problem with most salespeople is that they are order-takers and not trusted advisors. They know all about the product or service they are selling but very little about their customer's business or industry.

Consequently, when the customer wants to solve a problem, they don't think of your salespeople as the people to turn to.

What if your salespeople were actively educating customers on best practices, latest trends, industry dynamics, and available opportunities that could potentially increase their business?

Your salespeople would become very valuable to your customers and do more business with them.

Ultimately, what your customers want is value. You can give them that value and increase their likelihood of doing business with you by training your salespeople to become trusted advisors.

Find out how here: <insert page link>

Kind Regards,

<insert name>

Email 5

Subject Line: The Best Salespeople Think Like Doctors

Hi <insert name>

The medical doctor diagnoses the underlying problems of a patient by asking a series of questions, making observations, and being well informed and educated. The doctor knows that prescription without diagnosis is malpractice.

Yet, many salespeople are performing business malpractice by offering solutions to their customers without first uncovering their customers' needs.

The best salespeople act like doctors. They conduct extensive diagnoses of their client's real problems by asking intelligent questions and seeking to understand the underlying issues confronting their business.

If your salespeople are writing prescriptions without diagnosing the problem, they are doing your customers a disservice.

Help your salespeople think like doctors. Help them to transition from transactional salespeople to trusted advisors.

For more information on how to make the transition, visit <insert page link>

Kind Regards,

<insert name>

Email 6

Subject Line: *Like Sonulus HMO, You Can Recover Lost Accounts*

Customers leave when they are no longer receiving value from a company. Anyone can take orders—it's trusted advisors that can make your salesforce stand out.

But transitioning your salespeople into trusted advisors can be challenging.

Here's how Chris Montgomery, MD with Sonulus HMO, closed that gap:

"We were having problems getting our salespeople to sell in a consultative manner that would significantly improve the value we were giving our customers. We reached out to ActiveLearning to help us close the gaps between what our salespeople were doing and what would actually generate results.

ActiveLearning designed a program to help our salespeople make the transition from transactional salespeople to trusted advisors. Within three months, we were able to recover three previously lost or dormant accounts, grow our customer base by 3%, and our revenue went up by 7%. We are now confident that we can continue on this growth trajectory. To us, this has been a successful and great experience."

For more information on how your company can close the gap, visit <insert page link>

Kind Regards,

<insert name>

Email 7

Subject Line: *Are all banks the same? Not this one.*

Are all banks the same? Not the Carlton Banking Group.

They anticipated a shift in the needs of their customers and changed their business model from a lending institution to one that provides customers with valuable advisory services.

But did they have the people, process, and technology needed to make the transition? Not exactly. It's a major shift to move from being transactional to taking an advisory approach in sales, and not many companies know how to do it. That's where ActiveLearning was able to help.

At ActiveLearning, we are skilled and experienced at helping companies make the essential transition from transactional to advisory sales.

Using our 5D Methodology (Diagnose, Design, Develop, Deliver, Drive), we quickly identified a deficiency in the ability of Carlton Banking Group employees to provide professional advice to corporate clients. We also identified a gap in strategic thinking and industry knowledge. And a detailed plan to address these gaps was created and executed.

The results for the Carlton Banking Group? Improved client engagement, higher sales conversion rates, lower customer churn rates, and increased market share.

For more information on how ActiveLearning can help your company, contact <insert name and email>

Kind Regards,

<insert name>

Step 8 – Implement your marketing strategy

Once Elizabeth had carefully put Steps 1 to 7 in place, she launched her marketing campaign. She consistently published industry-relevant articles on LinkedIn and on her website. She promoted her lead magnet, the PDF guide she had created, to sales executives, senior heads of HR and Training. Through these channels, she generated quality leads whom she followed up using email and direct messaging.

She organised a webinar to teach at a deeper level the insights she had shared in her PDF guide. She promoted the webinar through her email sequence and via social media posts on LinkedIn and Twitter. Thirty-eight people attended the webinar and five asked her to submit a proposal. She was able to close two of those and she won her first business contract within a month of launching her marketing campaign.

By the end of the fourth month, she had been booked to deliver twelve training programs worth $60,000 to the business.

Whichever training pathway you choose to follow, like Elizabeth you will benefit significantly by learning to effectively market yourself and your offers. This is so important. You must be committed to creating and implementing a marketing strategy that will consistently get customers through the door.

Key Takeaways

- Marketing is the lifeblood of a business. The right marketing leads to sales, and without sales there is no business.

- The only reason you are in business is to serve your customers. Prioritise them by creating and improving your product based on market research.

- Focus on winning in the marketplace. No matter how great your product is, you still have the crucial responsibility of ensuring the right people see it and buy it.

- Marketing occurs in four stages. One, identifying the market's unfulfilled needs and desires. Two, defining the size of the identified market and its profit potential. Three, pinpointing how best to serve that need. And four, promoting the appropriate products and services to meet that need.

- Many businesses equate marketing with advertising. Running adverts is only one component of the marketing process, which is an intricate web of creative ideas, tactics, strategies, and actions.

11

YOU MUST CREATE YOUR ONLINE COURSE EMPIRE

"Too many people are thinking of security instead of opportunity. They seem more afraid of life than death."
James F. Byrnes

The COVID-19 pandemic has fundamentally altered the way we work, learn and relate with each other. People are open now, more than ever, to working and learning in a virtual environment, thereby creating an unprecedented opportunity for online course creators. With restrictions in travel and many adults working from home, the availability of online courses that can train people to do just about anything within the comfort of their home is no longer an option.

The global e-learning market is projected to be worth about $275 billion by 2022, and there has never been a better time for experts to leverage their expertise and experience to create online courses that could help thousands of people become successful, whilst generating a steady income for themselves.

As a Trainer, online courses are also a proven revenue generating model that can complement your in-person training programs in a number of ways. One, you can quickly establish yourself as an expert and thought leader in your field by creating well designed online courses that provide solutions to the problems in your niche market.

Two, you can multiply your revenue, reach and impact by making it possible for customers to access your content at any time of the day, as well as giving those who cannot attend your in-person training due to distance or other physical limitations the flexibility to still benefit from your expertise.

Three, online courses can be used as an effective, low-cost marketing tool that gives your target market the opportunity to experience a scaled down version of a high-end training program. Prospective customers who are still undecided about you or the effectiveness of your training program might be more willing to pay for a lower-cost introductory mini course on the subject.

> *It is a well-known fact that it is easier to keep a customer than to acquire a new one.*

Lastly, online courses can be used as a post-training tool to maintain a profitable relationship with your customers. It is a well-known fact that it is easier to keep a customer than to acquire a new one. An online course that builds on the knowledge, skill or competence taught during an in-person training is a great way to move clients towards the next step in their learning journey with you.

"Education is improving the lives of others and leaving your community and your world better than you found it."
Marian Wright Edelman

To create an online course, there are seven steps you must follow. As with any worthy venture, creating a successful online course requires a well-crafted plan and the use of the right tools and resources. With the plethora of choices available out there, this can be quite confusing and frustrating. That is why I have created an online course to guide you step by step through everything you need to create and sell your online course. Find out more about this course at youmustbecomeatrainer.com/create-your-online-course.

Step 1 – Choose an appropriate course topic

This is the first and most important step in creating your online course. In Chapter 6, I walked you through the process of selecting your niche market. Use this to help you choose the right topic for your online course. Focus on delivering a course that caters for the needs of your target customers, balanced with the areas you are most passionate about. Your goal ultimately, is to create the right course, at the right time, for the right people, at the right cost to help them achieve the right results. This includes identifying a subject matter that your target market is motivated enough to pay for. People will only purchase your course when they see it is a solution to a specific problem they are facing. And, to give your course the best chance at becoming successful, your area of focus must be as specific as possible. Creating a course that appeals to everyone will appeal to no one.

People will only purchase your course when they see it is a solution to a specific problem they are facing.

Step 2 – Validate your course topic

Until you expose your idea to market feedback, there are no guarantees whatsoever that it will do well. It is easy to assume based on your own convictions that you have found exactly what the market needs. But until you validate that idea by testing the market, you risk losing the time, energy and money you invested in creating a course that resonates with no one.

Validating your course topic can be as simple as surveying your target market using tools such as Google Forms or Typeform. Ask what their most pressing challenges are and gauge their willingness to invest in solving the problems you identified in the previous step. Another way is to test the profit potential of the course by pre-selling it before you create the full course. That way, you can cut your losses and shelve the idea if no one, or a significantly smaller number than you had projected, shows interest in the course. Even if market research reveals that there is sufficient interest in the course, time and care must be taken to incorporate the feedback when creating the course.

Step 3 – Plan your course content

After you have gathered enough evidence that there is a market demand for your course topic, you are now ready to create your online course. This is where the bulk of the work will be done. One major advantage of online courses is that you only have to create the content once.

The first step is to write out compelling learning objectives that clearly lay out what students would know, how they would feel or what they would be able to do by the end of your course. In addition to helping you streamline the content of your course, this process ensures that the right students enrol on your course. Refer to Chapter 7 for more details on how to write learning objectives.

Next, create an outline for the course content. The content outline or structure should make it easy for learning to flow in a logical sequence from one section to the next. This is where a detailed knowledge of your target market proves valuable. If you can identify the gap between the current situation and the desired outcomes of your potential students, you can tailor the content to begin right where they are and skilfully provide them with the training content they require to reach their goals. Begin with the end (the desired outcomes) and work backwards through each stage of the learning journey to identify the prerequisite knowledge they need to be successful at each stage. These clusters of content then become building blocks that guide students to their desired outcomes.

Group the building blocks into modules and units. On average, each module should contain a similar number of units and be of a similar time duration. To ensure proper grouping, modules should be independent enough to stand alone, and should answer a specific question along the learning journey.

Once you have created a sequential outline for your course, distil the vast amount of knowledge and information you have gathered on that subject matter to create content that will effectively help your students achieve the proposed outcomes. You should not only look out for what needs to be included but also what needs to be left out. The in-depth knowledge of your target market gained from your market research will help you narrow down your content to what actually addresses your customers' needs and to weed out the fluff. Align the content to each of the learning outcomes, and any material that is not clearly matched to an outcome should be left out of the course. This will help you avoid information overload.

In Chapter 8, I shared several insights into the unique ways that adults learn and why it is crucial to identify the most effective and engaging ways to deliver your course content. Aim to use instructional methods that will encourage students to remain engaged throughout the course. Online course content can be delivered using videos, audios, PDFs, case studies, quizzes, articles and

Find the instructional methods that work best for your target audience

much more. Find the instructional methods that work best for your target audience and more importantly, try to use a variety so that you can cater for different learning styles.

Step 4 – Create your course content

Once you have designed a detailed course outline and settled on the right training delivery strategy, it is time to create the content. Videos are the most popular delivery method nowadays and I will focus on that in this book.

When using videos, you can either record yourself delivering the content on screen, or you could use screencast, which is a digital recording of text or images displayed on your screen as you talk through the presentation. At the very least, you need a laptop with an in-built camera and microphone to record your content. For higher quality videos, it is worth investing in more advanced recording equipment such as digital cameras.

As you record, it is important to bear in mind that you are selling more than information. You are also selling the conviction that the content will help the student.

As you record, it is important to bear in mind that you are selling more than information. You are also selling the conviction that the content will help the student. Therefore, you must present the information in a passionate and entertaining manner that will inspire students to stay engaged and take immediate action. Remind them continuously of the benefits of taking action. Start each lesson with an enticing reminder of what they will achieve by implementing your content. Use effective storytelling to evoke an emotional response that will connect you to your learners.

Once you are done recording, edit your videos to be the best possible version you can achieve without getting bogged down with trying to achieve perfection. You can always recreate the videos later based on feedback from your students. The length of your videos should be appropriate to the lessons being taught; split long videos into shorter parts to maintain engagement.

Step 5 - Host your online course

Once your content is created, next, you will host it on an online platform to allow students and potential buyers access it easily. There are three major ways to do this. You could host it yourself by setting up a website and a payment processing system on a platform such WordPress, Wix, or Squarespace. This method requires you to have significant technical know-how. You also have the option of hiring a web developer to build it for you.

You could use online course marketplaces such as Udemy and Coursera. In this case, you only need to upload your content and every other process is done for you. This is by far the easiest way to get started as an online course creator. You will, however, be subject to restrictions that could limit your control over important elements such as course structure and pricing.

Use effective storytelling to evoke an emotional response that will connect you to your learners.

Lastly, there are Learning Management Systems (LMS) such as Didemy, Kajabi, Thinkific and Teachable. These platforms are a good midpoint between building your own website and using a course marketplace. You have more flexibility in designing your course, and because they are easier to set up than a bespoke website, you can usually do it yourself.

Step 6 - Determine your pricing model

Your online course can serve multiple purposes – as a lead magnet; an additional income stream; or a customer retention tool. This should, therefore, determine the type of course you create and how much you charge for it. It is advisable to research the market thoroughly and analyse your competitors' online course offerings when deciding the price of your course. As the popularity or impact of your online course increases, you can adjust your prices accordingly. Your online course can either be sold for a one-time payment, which is suitable for standalone courses, or as a subscription where new content is uploaded regularly for a recurring fee.

Step 7 – Create a marketing plan

As repeatedly emphasised in Chapter 10, your online course will fail if people do not buy it. Invest a considerable amount of time into researching the best ways to market your course to generate sales. Be intentional about devising a marketing plan that will make your online course stand out in the marketplace and attract your target audience. This could include the use of email marketing, advertisements, affiliate marketing, and social media promotions. Study Chapter 10 for more ideas on how to create your marketing strategy.

Creating a relevant, timely and well-designed online course is a brilliant way to broaden your impact, break your income ceiling and grow your visibility as a leader in your field of expertise. The seven steps highlighted above are a fail-safe strategy that, if combined with the right knowledge, tools and know-how, will help you achieve your goal of becoming a successful online course creator.

To help shorten your journey, I have created a companion course that will take you step by step through everything you need to create and sell your online course. Find out more at **www. youmustbecomeatrainer.com/create-your-online-course**.

Key Takeaways

- Online courses are a global multi-billion-dollar industry. There has never been a better time to leverage your expertise as an online course creator to help thousands of people and generate a steady income without ever leaving your home.

- To create a highly successful online course, there are seven steps that you must follow. One, choose an appropriate course topic that is well-matched to your area of expertise and has a high market demand.

- Two, validate your online course topic or idea by exposing it to market feedback.

- Three, plan your online course in great detail, including how the content will be structured and the delivery methods you will use.

- Four, create the course content using a variety of your chosen instructional methods.

- Five, choose the appropriate platform to host your course.

- Six, design your pricing model based on the purpose of the course and industry prices.

- Seven, create a robust marketing plan to launch your course and generate sales.

YOU **MUST** BECOME A **TRAINER**

CONCLUSION

YOU MUST BE THE BEST AND SUCCEED

"No matter how good you get you can always get better, and that's the exciting part."
Tiger Woods

Throughout this book, I have tried my best to show you why becoming a Trainer is a great career or business choice and how it can be a real game-changer for your financial future. However, for training to have that kind of impact on your life and on the people and organisations you serve, you must be willing to do it passionately and excellently. You cannot be average as a Trainer and expect to reap the rewards described in this book. To stand out as a Trainer, to achieve the kind of success that leaves a legacy, you must be excellent at it.

> *You cannot be average as a Trainer and expect to reap the rewards described in this book.*

So, what does it take to become an excellent Trainer? In my bid to ensure that everyone who reads this book gets everything they need to become successful a Trainer, I carried out extensive research into the factors that distinguish the most successful Trainers from those operating and earning at an average level. Listed below are the top 10 non-negotiable skills and qualities you must pursue as you build your career or business in training.

i. **Learn from the best.** Find and engage the services of a coach or mentor.

ii. **Work for the best.** If you have the opportunity to work for world-class organisations that are really good at training, it can be an invaluable experience for your future career or business.

iii. **Link with the best.** Network and make new connections always. Become better at strategic networking. Being active in a professional training community, whether online or in person, will help you stay up to date with industry news and provide you with access to peers you can bounce ideas off.

iv. **Partner and collaborate with the best as a deliberate growth strategy.** Great things happen when people of like mind work together towards a common goal. By each person contributing their own specialism, they will increase the overall rate of performance.

v. **Position yourself as the best.** Become a visible expert. No matter how good you are, if nobody or very few people know about you, your impact will be severely limited.

vi. **Hire the best.** Hiring the wrong person or people can destroy overnight what you carefully built over time. You must get your hiring right. I recommend my book, *Hiring Right – A Matter of Life and Death for Businesses, Business Owners and Executives*, to help with this.

vii. **Deliver the best service.** Follow through and deliver on your promises to clients. Your education, training, and credentials mean nothing if you cannot deliver results to clients. Therefore, your primary focus must always be on providing solutions to your clients' problems. Sometimes, what the client asks you to do is not an effective strategy, so you need to educate them on the best course of action that would generate the desired results.

viii. **Learn to be the best.** Study, study, and study – you cannot give what you do not have. Invest in continuous learning and personal development. To keep growing as a Trainer, from time to time, you will need to step out of your comfort zone. For example, you may be reluctant to use a new and unfamiliar program, but if you invest the time required to learn more about it, you may find that it increases your effectiveness as a Trainer.

ix. **Create the best experience for yourself and your learners**. Training is not just standing in front of a room and going through the training content. You need to connect with your trainees and make sure they are engaged. Engagement makes it more likely for them to internalise the information and be successful with what they are learning. And it is a lot easier to keep your trainees engaged when they are enjoying the experience. Asking questions during the training or including practical exercises will keep your trainees from zoning out. Cracking a witty jab from time to time can go a long way too!

x. **Remain the best by being dynamic and adaptable**. Even if your content stays the same, you can alter or vary your delivery to keep things fresh and interesting. Every group you teach will be made up of unique individuals who have different learning needs. Take the time to learn what works best for them based on their demographics and learning styles, and adapt your training programs accordingly.

"Teachers have three loves: love of learning, love of learners, and the love of bringing the first two loves together."
Scott Hayden

There you have it; my top ten non-negotiable tips to take with you on your journey to the top. Thank you for reading my book. I hope you gleaned a lot of insight and guidance from it. And more importantly, I hope you act on what you have learnt to create training programs that will impact the world and generate the income you need to be financially free and live your best life. Here is wishing you great success on your journey to becoming a sought after and phenomenally successful Trainer.

THE BEGINNING

Start Building Your Training
Empire, Today!

Visit
OwnersInstitute.com

APPENDICES

APPENDIX 1

101 HIGHLY INTERESTING AND SUCCESSFUL EXAMPLES OF TRAINING NICHES

Below are some examples of successful niches in training to stimulate your thinking and inspire you in the process of coming up with your own.

1. Gordon Ramsay Teaches Cooking

2. David Mamet Teaches Dramatic Writing

3. Billy Collins Teaches Reading and Writing Poetry

4. Ron Howard Teaches Directing

5. Margaret Atwood Teaches Creative Writing

6. Hans Zimmer Teaches Film Scoring

7. Phil Ivey Teaches Poker Strategy

8. Bob Woodward Teaches Investigative Journalism

9. erena Williams Teaches Tennis

10. Alice Waters Teaches the Art of Home Cooking

11. Usher Teaches the Art of Performance

12. Frank Gehry Teaches Design and Architecture

13. Will Wright Teaches Game Design and Theory

14. Aaron Sorkin Teaches Screenwriting

15. Natalie Portman Teaches Acting

16. Spike Lee Teaches Independent Filmmaking

17. Jimmy Chin Teaches Adventure Photography

18. Dominique Ansel Teaches French Pastry Fundamentals

19. Massimo Bottura Teaches Modern Italian Cooking

20. Martin Scorsese Teaches Filmmaking

21. Paul Krugman Teaches Economics and Society

22. Thomas Keller Teaches Cooking Techniques Part I: Vegetables, Pasta, and Eggs

23. Judy Blume Teaches Writing

24. Samuel L. Jackson Teaches Acting

25. Aaron Franklin Teaches Texas-Style BBQ

26. Annie Leibovitz Teaches Photography

27. Steve Martin Teaches Comedy

28. Shonda Rhimes Teaches Writing for Television

29. Howard Schultz Teaches Business Leadership

30. Jodie Foster Teaches Filmmaking

31. Ken Burns Teaches Documentary Filmmaking

32. Dr. Jane Goodall Teaches Conservation

33. Daniel Negreanu Teaches Poker

34. Mira Nair Teaches Independent Filmmaking

35. Werner Herzog Teaches Filmmaking

36. Stephen Curry Teaches Shooting, Ball-Handling, and Scoring

37. Malcolm Gladwell Teaches Writing

38. Thomas Keller Teaches Cooking Techniques Part II: Meats, Stocks, and Sauces

39. Diane von Furstenberg Teaches Building a Fashion Brand

40. Usher Teaches the Art Of Performance

41. R.L. Stine Teaches Writing for Young Audiences

42. David Lynch Teaches Creativity and Film

43. Marc Jacobs Teaches Fashion Design

44. Dan Brown Teaches Writing Thrillers

45. Wolfgang Puck Teaches Cooking

46. Judd Apatow Teaches Comedy

47. Timbaland Teaches Producing and Beatmaking

48. Helen Mirren Teaches Acting

49. Chris Hadfield Teaches Space Exploration

50. Karl Rove and David Axelrod Teach Campaign Strategy and Messaging

51. Massimo Bottura Teaches Modern Italian Cooking

52. James Patterson Teaches Writing

53. Fast Track Entrepreneur: Build an Online Business in 4 Weeks

54. Earn Passive Income by Working from Home with Google Adsense

55. How to Make A Great First Impression

56. Write Better Emails: Tactics for Smarter Team Communication

57. Advanced Communication Skills for 21st Century Leaders

58. Persuasion Masterclass: How to Powerfully Influence Anyone

59. Start a Successful Social Media Marketing Agency from Home

60. How to Succeed At Interviews

61. Start Writing Fiction

62. Research Writing: How to Do a Literature Review

63. Business Fundamentals: Effective Networking

64. Food as Medicine: Fertility and Pregnancy

65. Introduction to Chinese: Grammar

66. Harnessing Cultural Diversity: Effective Team Leadership in the Workplace

67. Hotel Revenue Management: The Strategy and Tactics of Hotel Room Pricing

68. Cognitive Behavioural Skills to Treat Back Pain: The Back Skills Training (BaST) Program

69. Learn Jazz Piano: II. Improvising on Jazz Standards

70. Talking About Cancer: Reducing Risk, Early Detection and Myth Busting

71. How to Understand Addiction

72. Storytelling in Advertising

73. Youth Football Coaching: Developing Creative Players

74. Numeracy Skills for Employability and the Workplace

75. An Introduction to Public Leadership

76. Prepare for Career Success at University

77. Basic First Aid: How to Be an Everyday Hero

78. How to Read Your Boss

79. Digital Discovery 1: Build Your Confidence Online

80. Career Credentials: Evidence Your Expertise in Teamwork

81. World of Spies: Keeping Secrets

82. Mario Botta: To Be an Architect

83. Could You Be the Next Florence Nightingale?

84. Creating an Online Video Ad: 1 Writing, Production, and Shooting

85. How to Detect a Lie

86. How to Escape a Kidnapper as an Adult

87. How to Do Coin & Card Magic Tricks with Jason Suran

88. How to Draw Fashion Sketches

89. Easy Fondant Cake Decorations for Kid Bakers

90. The Essential Guide to Remote Working - Master Freedom of Time & Make Technology Your Slave

91. Be a Self-Employed Massage or Bodywork Professional

92. Living Abroad Successfully: All the Ingredients You Need to Plan. Then, GO!

93. Anatomy of a Winning Proposal

94. Communicate Like a Boss

95. Manners @ The Table: A Modern Guide to Dining Etiquette

96. Beginner's Guide to Investing

97. What the Most Successful People Do Before Breakfast

98. Create a Hiring Plan & Grow Your Standout Business

99. How to Budget and Save Money

100. How to Pay Off Your Debt

101. Lose Weight Without Dieting

APPENDIX 2

ELIZABETH'S LEAD GENERATING PDF: THE KEY TO WINNING MORE BUSINESS (AND KEEPING IT)

Are your salespeople struggling to attract, retain, and grow key accounts?

Is your company underperforming relative to its vast potential and market opportunities?

If so, your salespeople may be transactional, meaning they are simply focused on taking orders rather than helping your customers solve their problems. Eventually, you will lose customers to a competitor who can help them solve their problems.

The key to winning more business is transitioning your salespeople from a transactional mindset to become trusted advisors.

What are the key attributes of a successful, trusted advisor? How do you make the transition from transactional to trusted?

For the last 15 years, we have worked with companies to help answer these questions, training over 1200 salespeople. We recently conducted a survey of about 178 key decision makers across medium and large scale organisations to learn what they love the most about the salespeople whose advice they value, to whom they entrust their businesses and whose services they enthusiastically recommend. What we discovered are seven important attributes that your salespeople must possess if they are to attract, retain, and grow key clients.

1. Trusted advisors have a deep understanding of their customer's business

    - The best trusted advisors have in-depth understanding of their client's business realities.

    - They understand that business success is determined by internal and external realities, and they go out of their way to gain a deep understanding of the specific challenges their client are facing, as well as the opportunities available to their business.

    - They apply this knowledge to help their clients win in their business space.

2. They educate clients by sharing relevant knowledge & insights

    - The best sales advisors educate their clients.

    - They leverage their experience to serve clients in diverse industries, as well as research findings to educate clients on latest trends, industry dynamics, and mind-the-gap issues that can have adverse effects on the client's business.

    - They help their clients stay on top of their business and industry by sharing articles, white papers, research reports, etc.

    - They help their clients see around the corner and prepare for the unknown.

- They actively source for and notify clients on relevant opportunities they can explore to help their business grow.

3. They demonstrate strong business and financial acumen

- The best trusted advisors demonstrate a firm grasp of business fundamentals and financial acumen.

- They speak the language of business and help clients clarify their thinking in key areas such as business modelling, strategy, finance, etc.

- They serve as the go-to person on crucial finance and other business-related issues.

4. They possess excellent knowledge of their products and services

- The best trusted advisors have excellent knowledge of their products and services and how they fit into the client's needs.

- They understand the problems they are solving for clients and are able to tailor their offering to meet the client's needs.

- This knowledge enables them to offer suitable options, highlighting the pros and cons where applicable, and providing unbiased advice on critical decisions.

5. They are consummate professionals

- The best trusted advisors are professionals to their core. They keep to time, honour appointments and renegotiate deadlines they will not be able to meet.

- They follow through and do not promise what they cannot deliver – promises made are promises kept.

- They get things done and act with an appropriate sense of urgency.

- They provide updates and feedback without being prompted.

- They have the right level of exposure and experience.

6. They truly care and genuinely want their clients to succeed

   - The best trusted advisors care deeply about their clients and want to see their businesses succeed.

   - They make clients feel like they are very important to them as an individual.

   - They make the client's business a priority, consistently going beyond the call of duty to support them.

   - They are empathetic, humble, and exude an infectious level of self-confidence.

   - They take time to listen deeply and understand their clients. They don't take a one-size-fits-all approach in handling their client's business.

7. They ask the right questions and uncover the clients' needs

   - The best trusted advisors act like medical doctors.

   - They know that prescription without diagnosis is malpractice.

   - They carry out an extensive diagnosis to uncover their client's real issues by asking intelligent questions and seeking to understand the underlying problems confronting their clients.

Now that you know the attributes, how do you transition your salespeople into trusted advisors? We have developed a workshop to solve this problem: Making the Transition from Traditional Salesperson to Trusted Advisor. In this workshop, your salespeople will learn how to:

- Acquire profitable customers

- Achieve customer loyalty and retention

- Shorten sales cycles and reduce competitive threats

- Effectively cross-sell and expand relationships

- Engage at senior or C-Suite levels

Help your salespeople make this transition by:

- Signing up and attending the workshop

- Becoming a trusted advisor

- Winning business for your organisation

Don't waste another day with transactional salespeople.

Register today at **www.activelearning.com/trustedadvisorworkshop**.

ABOUT OWNERS INSTITUTE

At Owners Institute, we're on a mission to grow the next generation of Owners and Ownership-driven enterprises in Africa. We exist to help Individuals and Businesses in Africa realize their full potential.

Owners Institute is a pragmatic business school (minus the academic theories) for Established Entrepreneurs who want to grow their business, Employees who want to make the transition to Emerging Entrepreneurs/Intrapreneurs and Enterprising Experts who want to monetize their expertise by starting their own side hustle.

Too many businesses are failing at astronomical rates across Africa. The ones that are still in operation are struggling or mediocre at best. Likewise, individuals are underachieving relative to their potentials. We believe this should definitely not be the case. Owners Institute exists to help increase the odds of success of businesses, their owners or would-be owners.

We are a community-based platform that provides practical training, tools, coaching and support for Individuals and Businesses within our vibrant communities to enable them beat the odds and succeed where others are struggling.

Visit **www.ownersinstitute.com** to get started

Tweet at us: **@owners_Inst**

Send a DM: **OwnersInstitute_**

Connect on LinkedIn: **Owners Institute**

Follow on Facebook: **Owners Institute**

Send a mail: **oteam@ownersinstitute.com**

We care about you.
We want you to succeed.

ABOUT THE AUTHOR

Bolaji Olagunju is a Serial Entrepreneur, Author, Trainer, Coach and Consultant to some of the most important and interesting businesses in Africa.

He is the Founder and Executive Chairman of Workforce Group (www. workforcegroup.com) – one of the leading Business & HR Consulting firms in Africa made up of multiple subsidiaries offering business advisory, learning & development, outsourcing, recruitment & assessment, and market entry & operations support. Workforce Group has a staff strength of over 8000 people, and presence in 7 African countries and its headquarters are situated at The Zone (www.thezone.ng), a world-class purpose-built facility hired out to businesses for serviced private offices, meetings, training, hybrid conferences, retreats, strategy sessions, team building and corporate events.

Bolaji is also the Founder of Ownersinstitute.com, a pragmatic membership-based learning and growth community for Established and Emerging business owners and Subject Matter Experts who want to leverage their expertise to create wealth and build their business empire. And a co-founder in several technology start-ups including Learnry (a Learning Management System), Outwork (a task management solution), AllDay HR (a Human Resource Software for large corporations and SMEs) and mAudition (an innovative video application designed purely for entertainment).

He is an alumnus of London Business School and has attended several programs in leading universities all over the world including

Berkeley Haas School of Business, Colombia Business School, Michigan Ross Business School, Kellogg Business School, and UNC Kenan- Flagler Business School.

In 2019, Bolaji wrote the widely-acclaimed best-selling book – *Hiring Right: A Matter of Life and Death for Businesses, Business Owners and Executives* (www.hiringrightbook.com) which has been continuously lauded as the most practical manual for hiring employees in Africa.

He is passionate about learning, teaching, job creation, making people employable and mentoring entrepreneurs. In just a few short years, he transformed Workforce Management Centre into Workforce Group, made up of more than 6 subsidiaries and grew the business to multiple-seven figures in revenue. Together with his team of 20+ people spread all over the world, he now leads a mission to support a very special global community of 10,000+ loyal and inspired entrepreneurs.